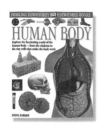 **DORLING KINDERSLEY EYEWITNESS BOOKS — HUMAN BODY**

 **HURRICANE & TORNADO**

 **INSECT**

 **INVENTION**

 **JUNGLE**

 **LIGHT**

 **MAMMAL**

 **MATTER**

 **MEDIA & COMMUNICATION**

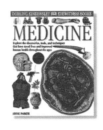 **MEDICINE**

 **MEDIEVAL LIFE**

 **MONEY**

 **MUMMY**

 **MUSIC**

 **MYTHOLOGY**

 **NORTH AMERICAN INDIAN**

 **OCEAN**

 **OLYMPICS**

 **PIRATE**

 **PLANT**

 **POND & RIVER**

 **PREHISTORIC LIFE**

 **PYRAMID**

 **RELIGION**

 **REPTILE**

 **RESCUE**

 **ROCKS & MINERALS**

 **SEASHORE**

 **SHARK**

 **SHELL**

 **SHIPWRECK**

 **SKELETON**

 **SOCCER**

 **SPACE EXPLORATION**

 **SPORTS**

 **SPY**

 **TECHNOLOGY**

 **TIME & SPACE**

 **TITANIC**

 **TRAIN**

 **TREE**

 **VIKING**

 **VOLCANO & EARTHQUAKE**

 **WEATHER**

 **WHALE**

 **WILD WEST**

 **WITCHES & MAGIC-MAKERS**

 **WORLD WAR I**

 **WORLD WAR II**

DORLING KINDERSLEY DK EYEWITNESS BOOKS

AMPHIBIAN

Tiger salamander

Underside of
neotenous alpine newt

European common frog
preparing for takeoff

Mantellas
showing color
variations

DK EYEWITNESS BOOKS

AMPHIBIAN

Written by
DR. BARRY CLARKE

Photographed by
GEOFF BRIGHTLING and
FRANK GREENAWAY

Mantellas

Crested
newt
tadpole

African
bullfrog

Dorling Kindersley

Skeleton of
Surinam
toad

Poison-dart frog

Dorling Kindersley

LONDON, NEW YORK, AUCKLAND, DELHI, JOHANNESBURG, MUNICH,
PARIS and SYDNEY

For a full catalog, visit

DK www.dk.com

Project editor Marion Dent
Art editor Jill Plank
Managing editor Helen Parker
Managing art editor Julia Harris
Production Louise Barratt
Picture research Clive Webster
Extra photography Mike Linley

This Eyewitness ® Book has been conceived by
Dorling Kindersley Limited and Editions Gallimard

© 1993 Dorling Kindersley Limited
This edition © 2000 Dorling Kindersley Limited
First American edition, 1993

Published in the United States by
Dorling Kindersley Publishing, Inc.
95 Madison Avenue
New York, NY 10016
2 4 6 8 10 9 7 5 3

Dorling Kindersley books are available at special discounts for bulk
purchases for sales promotions or premiums. Special editions, including
personalized covers, excerpts of existing guides, and corporate imprints
can be created in large quantities for specific needs. For more information,
contact Special Markets Dept., Dorling Kindersley Publishing, Inc.,
95 Madison Ave., New York, NY 10016; Fax: (800) 600-9098

Marine toad

Library of Congress Cataloging-in-Publication Data
Clarke, Barry.
Amphibian / written by Barry Clarke.
p. cm. — (Eyewitness Books)
Includes index.
Summary: Examines the evolution, behavior, physical
characteristics, and life cycle of all kinds of amphibians.
1. Amphibians — Juvenile literature.
[1. Amphibians.] I. Title.
QL644.2.C58 2000 597.6—dc20 92-1589
ISBN 0-7894-5755-5 (pb)
ISBN 0-7894-5754-7 (hc)

Color reproduction by Colourscan, Singapore
Printed in China by Toppan Printing Co. (Shenzhen) Ltd.

Red-eyed
tree frog
on leaf

Jeremy Fisher from
Beatrix Potter's
(1866–1943) *The Tale
of Mr. Jeremy Fisher*

Walking
sequence of a
tiger salamander

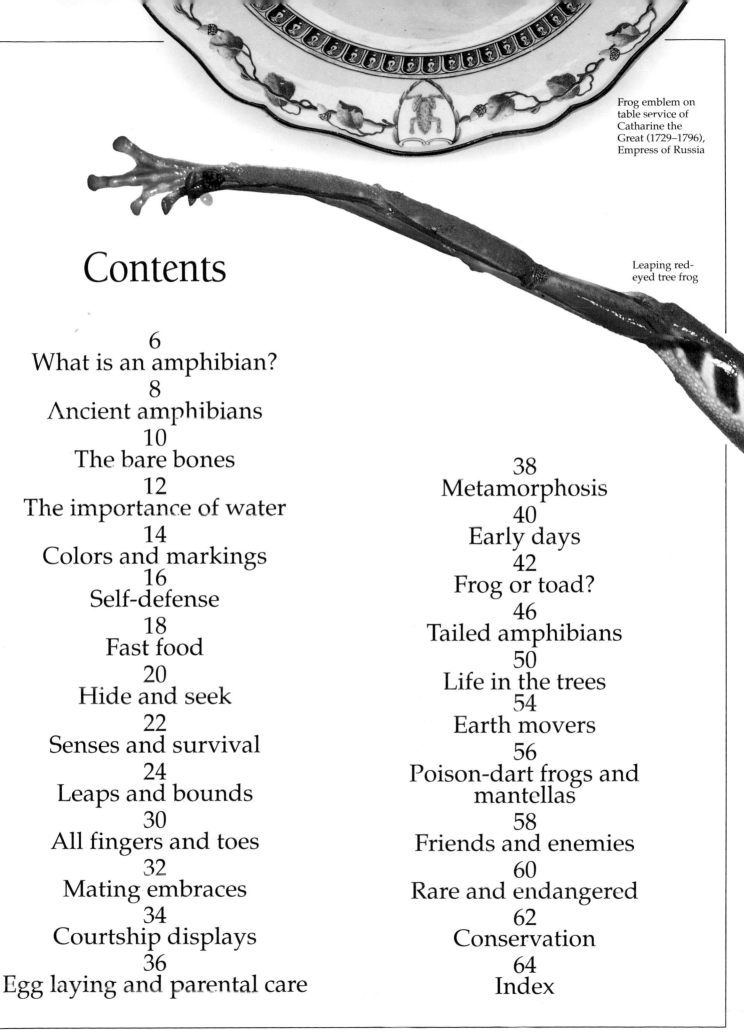

Leaping red-
eyed tree frog

Contents

What is an amphibian?

LIVING AMPHIBIANS are divided into three groups – frogs and toads; newts, salamanders, and sirens; and the little-known, wormlike caecilians. Amphibians are vertebrates (animals that have a backbone) like fish, reptiles, birds, and mammals. They are cold-blooded, which means that their body temperature varies with their surroundings. Unlike warm-blooded animals (mammals and birds), amphibians do not need to eat frequently to maintain their body temperature, so their food intake increases or decreases with their temperature and activity level. Amphibians have a naked skin (lacking hair, feathers, or surface scales) and can breathe through their skin as well as, or instead of, through their lungs.

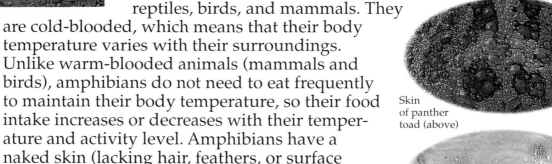

Skin of panther toad (above)

Skin of tree frog (right)

IN AND OUT OF WATER
This amphibious car can be driven on land or in water. The words "amphibious" and "amphibian" come from the Greek *amphi* and *bios* meaning "double life," that is, they can live or function on land and in water. Most amphibians pass from a free-living, aquatic (in water), larval stage into a terrestrial, or land-based, adult.

ONLY SKIN DEEP
An amphibian's skin is very special. Like all amphibians, frogs and toads use their skin to breathe through, lose or take up water, produce color patterns and markings for defense (pp. 20–21), and to attract a mate (pp. 32–33). They also secrete mucus from their skin to keep it moist and to protect it from being damaged.

A European common frog lives in woodlands close to water and ranges in length from 2.5–4 in (6–10 cm)

FROG-SHAPED
Frogs and toads (pp. 42–45) have a distinctive body shape – a large head with a wide mouth, prominent eyes, usually a fat body, no tail, back legs longer than the front ones, and an "extra" (third) heel section to the leg above the long foot. They probably evolved these features to chase, jump after, or lunge at insects on the move (pp. 18–19).

Smooth, slimy skin of frog is typical

Fire salamander's markings display polymorphism

What is not an amphibian?

This tegu lizard from the tropical parts of South America looks similar to a salamander, such as the fire salamander below, and some snakes, particularly the little worm snakes, look like caecilians, but lizards and snakes are reptiles, not amphibians. Reptiles can easily be told apart from amphibians by their dry, scaly skin. Earthworms and caecilians look very similar, but many a biologist has been startled to see the worm they had picked up open its mouth to show an impressive set of curved, sharp, little teeth! Also, some tadpoles look like small fish, but the lack of scales and body fins shows that they are quite different.

Skin of crested newt

Skin of orange striped newt

Tegu lizard – not an amphibian

Typical dry, scaly skin of reptile

THE ROUGH AND THE SMOOTH
Typically, newts have smooth, slimy skin and salamanders have dry, warty skin, but as with frogs and toads, there are always exceptions. For example, the fire salamander's skin (bottom) feels smooth and damp.

ODD AMPHIBIAN
The body rings on a caecilian make it look like a worm, but the shark-like head and needlesharp teeth show it is no worm! Some species have tiny, fishlike scales within the rings. About 170 species are found in tropical parts of the world.

Fire salamander lives in forests, but near water, and ranges in length from 6–13 in (15–32 cm)

Fire salamander's smooth, damp skin is typical of many amphibians

ANCESTRAL SHAPE
Newts and salamanders (pp. 46–49) are more like the early ancestral amphibians than either the more distinctive frogs and toads or the caecilians – the overall body shape has remained basically the same (pp. 8–9). The head is narrow and has small eyes and a smaller mouth than in frogs and toads; the body is long and lizard-shaped; and there is always a well-developed tail. Their four legs are all similar in size and length, so they walk slowly to moderately fast and catch slow-moving insects and earthworms for their food (pp. 18–19).

Ancient amphibians

TOAD IN THE HOLE
This toad is not a fossil – it is mummified. When it was tiny, the toad entered this hollow stone (found in England in the 1890s) via a small hole at one end, but eventually it died from a lack of food, water, and air.

THE FIRST AMPHIBIANS appeared on earth during the Devonian period some 360 million years ago. Their closest ancestors were fishes with fleshy, lobed fins that looked like legs. Some of these amphibians, like *Ichthyostega*, had fishlike features. Like their ancestors, they may have been attracted onto land by a good supply of food and fewer enemies to prey on them (pp. 58–59). Amphibians' ancestors had lungs for breathing air, and eventually their lobed fins developed into efficient walking limbs so they were able to walk around on land. Amphibians thrived from the Devonian to the Permian periods, when they were more varied in size and shape than they are today. *Diplocaulus*, for example, was quite small, but *Eryops* grew to 6.5 ft (2 m) or more. Most amphibians had become extinct by the Triassic period, leaving only a few – such as *Triadobatrachus* and *Rana pueyoi* – to evolve into modern amphibians (pp. 42–49).

Artist's reconstruction of *Triadobatrachus*

One half of *Triadobatrachus* fossil sandwich

Short hind leg

FISHY FINS
These are reconstructions of *Ichthyostega*, an early amphibian from the Devonian period in Greenland. It had some fishlike features, like a tail fin and small scales, in its distinctly amphibian body but had legs suitable for walking and fewer skull bones than a fish.

Skeleton of *Ichthyostega*

Reconstruction of *Ichthyostega*

TIME CHART OF THE EARTH				
PERIOD (MILLIONS OF YEARS AGO)	EARLY AMPHIBIANS	CAECILIANS	NEWTS, SALAMANDERS, AND SIRENS	FROGS AND TOADS
PALEOCENE TO PRESENT DAY (70)		Only caecilian fossil •		
CRETACEOUS (140)			Earliest known salamander	Earliest known frog
JURASSIC (190)			▽ •	▽ •
TRIASSIC (225)				•
PERMIAN (270)	*Eryops* •			*Triadobatrachus*
CARBONIFEROUS (350)	*Ichthyostega* •			
DEVONIAN (400)	⋙			

Duration of each period not to scale

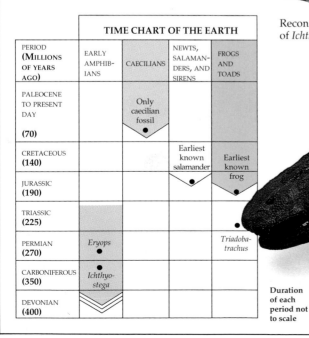

Sharp teeth of a meat eater

Skeleton of *Eryops*

AMPHIBIAN CROCODILE
This skeleton is of *Eryops*, a crocodilelike amphibian that lived in swamps in Texas during the Permian period. These terrestrial creatures used their strong limbs to move around on land.

Wide, flat skull, like modern frogs

Short tail

SLIM EVIDENCE
This fossil sandwich (above and left) is the only known specimen of *Triadobatrachus*, which was found in France dating from the Triassic period, about 210 million years ago. It has a wide, flat, froglike skull, but it also contains more vertebrae than modern frogs do, as well as a bony tail and short hind legs.

ANCIENT FROG
This 20-million-year-old fossil frog, *Discoglossus*, is from the Miocene period and was found in Germany. It is structurally similar to its close relative from the late Jurassic period, *Eodiscoglossus*, which was found in Spain. The modern living species of *Discoglossus* show that they have remained almost unchanged over the last 150 million years.

Outline of plump body

MORE MODERN FROG
Well-preserved fossil frog skeletons, like *Rana pueyoi* from the Miocene of Spain, are much like some modern European frogs that belong to the same genus, *Rana* (pp. 42–43). Fossil frogs like this help experts to date when modern frog groups first appeared. They also show how little some groups have changed in the 25 million years since the early Miocene period.

Fleshy, long hind leg

Long tail of fossil salamander is like that of modern hellbender

Short, stout leg supporting heavy body

ARROW-HEADED AMPHIBIAN
This odd-looking amphibian, found in Texas, is *Diplocaulus* (24 in, 60 cm long), a member of an extinct group that lived in Permian ponds.

RELATIVE FROM ABROAD
This fossil salamander, whose Latin name is *Cryptobranchus scheuchzeri*, was found in Switzerland and is about eight million years old. It is a close relative of the hellbender, *Cryptobranchus alleganiensis*, the only living member now living in the southeastern U.S. Fossils like this provide evidence that some amphibians, like these hellbenders (pp. 48–49), once had a much wider distribution and that landmasses that are now separate were once joined. Unfortunately, the fossil record is poor and their origins and relationship remain a mystery.

The bare bones

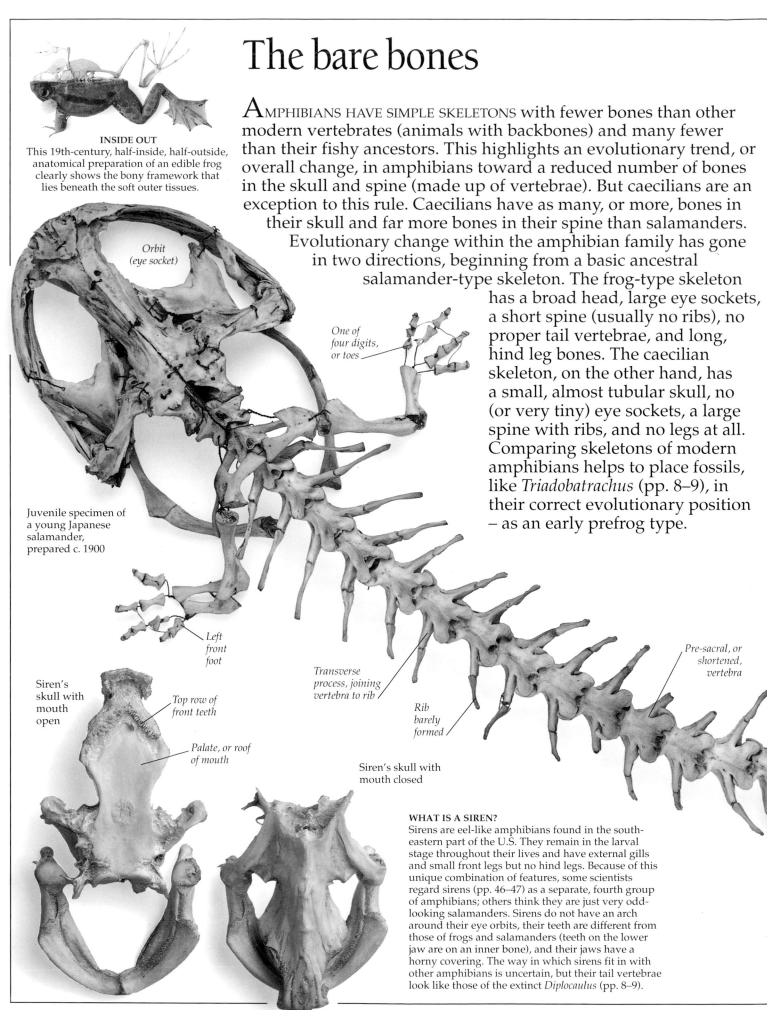

AMPHIBIANS HAVE SIMPLE SKELETONS with fewer bones than other modern vertebrates (animals with backbones) and many fewer than their fishy ancestors. This highlights an evolutionary trend, or overall change, in amphibians toward a reduced number of bones in the skull and spine (made up of vertebrae). But caecilians are an exception to this rule. Caecilians have as many, or more, bones in their skull and far more bones in their spine than salamanders. Evolutionary change within the amphibian family has gone in two directions, beginning from a basic ancestral salamander-type skeleton. The frog-type skeleton has a broad head, large eye sockets, a short spine (usually no ribs), no proper tail vertebrae, and long, hind leg bones. The caecilian skeleton, on the other hand, has a small, almost tubular skull, no (or very tiny) eye sockets, a large spine with ribs, and no legs at all. Comparing skeletons of modern amphibians helps to place fossils, like *Triadobatrachus* (pp. 8–9), in their correct evolutionary position – as an early prefrog type.

INSIDE OUT
This 19th-century, half-inside, half-outside, anatomical preparation of an edible frog clearly shows the bony framework that lies beneath the soft outer tissues.

Orbit (eye socket)

One of four digits, or toes

Juvenile specimen of a young Japanese salamander, prepared c. 1900

Left front foot

Siren's skull with mouth open

Top row of front teeth

Palate, or roof of mouth

Transverse process, joining vertebra to rib

Rib barely formed

Pre-sacral, or shortened, vertebra

Siren's skull with mouth closed

WHAT IS A SIREN?
Sirens are eel-like amphibians found in the south-eastern part of the U.S. They remain in the larval stage throughout their lives and have external gills and small front legs but no hind legs. Because of this unique combination of features, some scientists regard sirens (pp. 46–47) as a separate, fourth group of amphibians; others think they are just very odd-looking salamanders. Sirens do not have an arch around their eye orbits, their teeth are different from those of frogs and salamanders (teeth on the lower jaw are on an inner bone), and their jaws have a horny covering. The way in which sirens fit in with other amphibians is uncertain, but their tail vertebrae look like those of the extinct *Diplocaulus* (pp. 8–9).

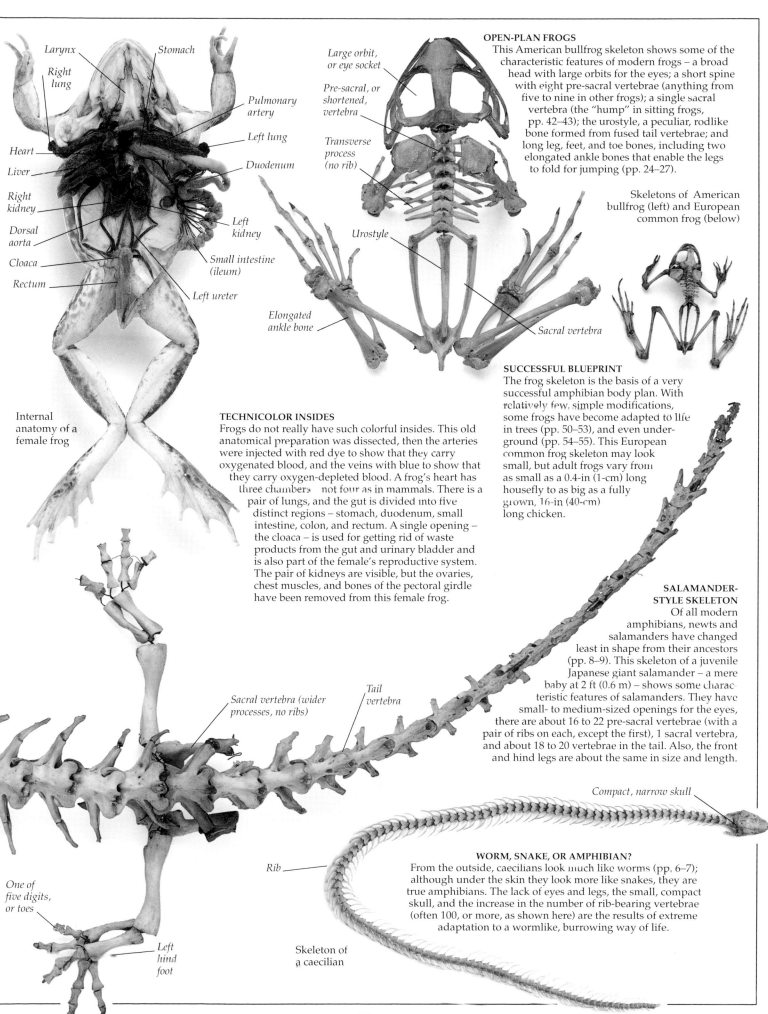

Larynx

Right lung

Stomach

Heart

Liver

Right kidney

Dorsal aorta

Cloaca

Rectum

Pulmonary artery

Left lung

Duodenum

Left kidney

Small intestine (ileum)

Left ureter

Internal anatomy of a female frog

OPEN-PLAN FROGS

This American bullfrog skeleton shows some of the characteristic features of modern frogs – a broad head with large orbits for the eyes; a short spine with eight pre-sacral vertebrae (anything from five to nine in other frogs); a single sacral vertebra (the "hump" in sitting frogs, pp. 42–43); the urostyle, a peculiar, rodlike bone formed from fused tail vertebrae; and long leg, feet, and toe bones, including two elongated ankle bones that enable the legs to fold for jumping (pp. 24–27).

Large orbit, or eye socket

Pre-sacral, or shortened, vertebra

Transverse process (no rib)

Urostyle

Elongated ankle bone

Sacral vertebra

Skeletons of American bullfrog (left) and European common frog (below)

TECHNICOLOR INSIDES

Frogs do not really have such colorful insides. This old anatomical preparation was dissected, then the arteries were injected with red dye to show that they carry oxygenated blood, and the veins with blue to show that they carry oxygen-depleted blood. A frog's heart has three chambers – not four as in mammals. There is a pair of lungs, and the gut is divided into five distinct regions – stomach, duodenum, small intestine, colon, and rectum. A single opening – the cloaca – is used for getting rid of waste products from the gut and urinary bladder and is also part of the female's reproductive system. The pair of kidneys are visible, but the ovaries, chest muscles, and bones of the pectoral girdle have been removed from this female frog.

SUCCESSFUL BLUEPRINT

The frog skeleton is the basis of a very successful amphibian body plan. With relatively few, simple modifications, some frogs have become adapted to life in trees (pp. 50–53), and even underground (pp. 54–55). This European common frog skeleton may look small, but adult frogs vary from as small as a 0.4-in (1-cm) long housefly to as big as a fully grown, 16-in (40-cm) long chicken.

SALAMANDER-STYLE SKELETON

Of all modern amphibians, newts and salamanders have changed least in shape from their ancestors (pp. 8–9). This skeleton of a juvenile Japanese giant salamander – a mere baby at 2 ft (0.6 m) – shows some characteristic features of salamanders. They have small- to medium-sized openings for the eyes, there are about 16 to 22 pre-sacral vertebrae (with a pair of ribs on each, except the first), 1 sacral vertebra, and about 18 to 20 vertebrae in the tail. Also, the front and hind legs are about the same in size and length.

Sacral vertebra (wider processes, no ribs)

Tail vertebra

Compact, narrow skull

One of five digits, or toes

Left hind foot

Rib

Skeleton of a caecilian

WORM, SNAKE, OR AMPHIBIAN?

From the outside, caecilians look much like worms (pp. 6–7); although under the skin they look more like snakes, they are true amphibians. The lack of eyes and legs, the small, compact skull, and the increase in the number of rib-bearing vertebrae (often 100, or more, as shown here) are the results of extreme adaptation to a wormlike, burrowing way of life.

The importance of water

WATER PLAYS A VITAL role in amphibian life. Amphibians need fresh water to keep their skin moist, and most species require a watery environment for reproduction – especially species that spend all or part of their lives as larvae under water. In aquatic or swampy habitats, water passes rapidly through an amphibian's skin into its body and has to be eliminated via its kidneys. In dry areas, amphibians risk losing more water than they can take up. Frogs can reduce water loss by having a less porous skin, by seeking damp, shady places, by burrowing, and by taking up water from wet surfaces. Some toads obtain almost three-quarters of the water they need through a "seat," or baggy patch, on their pelvis that they press against moist surfaces. Amphibians rarely drink water, although they may take in a little with their food. Many amphibians have adapted their behavior and skin surface structure to a surprising variety of habitats: to life in ponds and in trees (even high in the forest canopy where the only freestanding water collects in pockets formed by leaves), and to life in the desert, by burrowing and forming cocoons.

FLOWER POWER
Thumbelina is a children's story about a tiny flower fairy stolen by a toad who wanted Thumbelina to marry his ugly son. The old toad imprisoned Thumbelina on a lily pad in the middle of a river, but helped by the fishes, she escaped and eventually married the Prince of the Flower People.

SHIP OF THE DESERT
Contrary to popular opinion, camels do not store water in their humps (which are fat reserves), but drink large quantities of water to replace what they have lost.

BREATHING UNDERWATER
The larva of the tiger salamander uses its three pairs of large, feathery gills to breathe underwater. The deep red gills are rich in blood vessels, which absorb the dissolved air from the water.

Female crested newt

WET AND DRY
Crested newts spend most of the year on land, returning to the water to breed in the spring (pp. 40–41). In the water they shed their dry, warty skin for a smoother one.

One of three pairs of gills

Young tiger salamander with gills

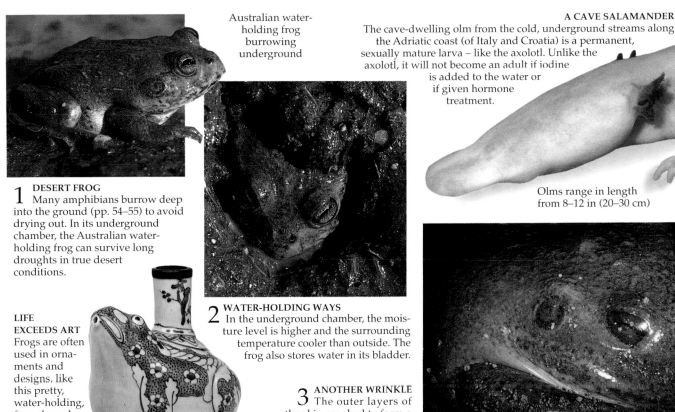

Australian water-holding frog burrowing underground

1 DESERT FROG
Many amphibians burrow deep into the ground (pp. 54–55) to avoid drying out. In its underground chamber, the Australian water-holding frog can survive long droughts in true desert conditions.

LIFE EXCEEDS ART
Frogs are often used in ornaments and designs, like this pretty, water-holding, frog-shaped flask, made in China during the 16th century.

2 WATER-HOLDING WAYS
In the underground chamber, the moisture level is higher and the surrounding temperature cooler than outside. The frog also stores water in its bladder.

3 ANOTHER WRINKLE
The outer layers of the skin are shed to form a cocoon, drastically reducing water loss. The frog emerges to feed and breed only when the rains come.

A CAVE SALAMANDER
The cave-dwelling olm from the cold, underground streams along the Adriatic coast (of Italy and Croatia) is a permanent, sexually mature larva – like the axolotl. Unlike the axolotl, it will not become an adult if iodine is added to the water or if given hormone treatment.

Olms range in length from 8–12 in (20–30 cm)

The adult will live on dry land in leaf litter or small burrows

California newt ranges in length from 5–8 in (13–20 cm)

Powerful back leg

Full webbing on foot

CALIFORNIA NEWT
This newt lays a clump of 12–24 eggs on underwater plants in late winter to early spring. Young newts leave the water in fall or early the following spring.

AN UNDERWATER LIFE
The African clawed toad spends most of its life in water, only coming onto land to migrate to nearby ponds or lakes (pp. 22–23). The flat head and body, powerful back legs, and fully webbed feet make this toad an excellent swimmer.

Red, feathery gills

Flat body

WATER BABY
In some species of newts and salamanders, larvae never change into adults, but remain in the water to become sexually mature in the larval state. This is known as "neoteny" (pp. 48–49). Neoteny may be caused by something in the environment – like low water temperature or a low level of iodine in the water. The axolotl (left) is the best known example of a neotenic larva.

Young albino (lacking color) African clawed toad

Axolotl

Colors and markings

AMPHIBIANS HAVE AN INCREDIBLE RANGE of colors and markings, from bright blues, reds, and yellows to muddy browns and greens, with a variety of stripes and spots. Many amphibians are darker on top, with a completely different color and pattern on their belly. Like most animals, amphibians either blend in with their surroundings for camouflage (pp. 20–21), or are brightly colored to show predators that they are poisonous to eat (pp. 56–57). An amphibian's color may also help absorb or reflect heat, or attract a mate (pp. 32–35). The main color and markings in an amphibian's skin are produced by three different color pigment cells – white, yellow, and brown-black – which are found deep in the skin. There is no green or blue pigment – a frog looks green when the blue part of white light is absorbed by yellow cells. Brown-black pigment cells can expand to darken, or contract to lighten, the animal's skin. An amphibian's color varies with humidity and temperature – it may become pale when warm and dry, darker if cold and damp.

THE FROG PRINCE
The story of the princess who kisses a frog, magically turning him into a handsome prince, is a well-known fairy tale. In the 1815 version by the Brothers Grimm, the princess dislikes the frog, but he tricks her into caring for him, breaking the wicked witch's spell.

White's tree frogs from Australia (above) and Indonesia (left)

Darker muddy green color

THE SAME BUT DIFFERENT ...
The intricate patterns on the upper surfaces of the head, body, arms, and legs of these two primarily green horned frogs from South America give them their common name of "ornate" horned frog (pp. 44–45). The small individual differences in skin colors and markings (left and below) are common within a species.

DARKEN DOWN, LIGHTEN UP!
A change in the background color of an amphibian is a response to changes in light, temperature, moisture, or even mood. Light green is the usual color for these White's tree frogs (pp. 50–51), but if they move away from a leaf's sunlit surface to a cool, shady, or damp place, they may change from green to light brown.

Enormous mouth for grabbing large prey

Short, sturdy leg

Pattern breaks up frog's shape

Three ornate horned frogs (left) from South America, – from 3.5–5 in (9–13 cm) long

DIFFERENT COLOR, DIFFERENT SPECIES
This brown form of horned frog (left) was thought to belong to the same species as the two green ones, but it was recognized as different in 1980. Although the pattern is similar, they are found in different, but nearby, habitats and do not interbreed in the wild. They are not polymorphic forms because they are not members of the same species.

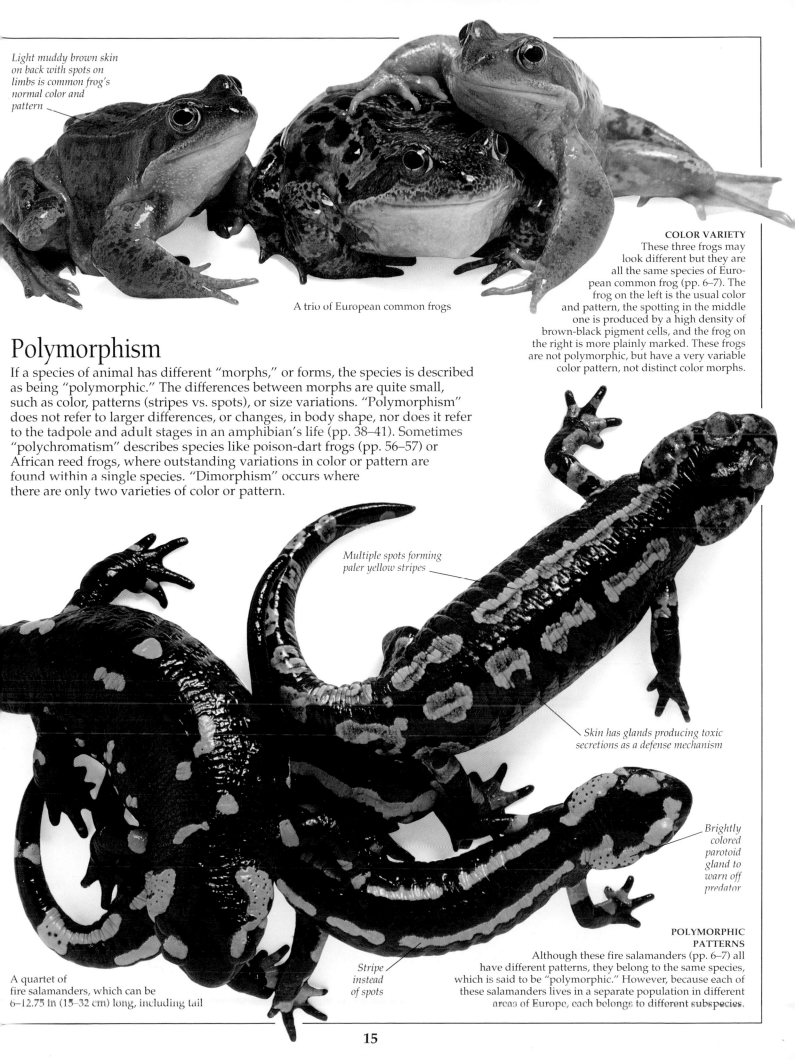

Light muddy brown skin on back with spots on limbs is common frog's normal color and pattern

A trio of European common frogs

COLOR VARIETY
These three frogs may look different but they are all the same species of European common frog (pp. 6–7). The frog on the left is the usual color and pattern, the spotting in the middle one is produced by a high density of brown-black pigment cells, and the frog on the right is more plainly marked. These frogs are not polymorphic, but have a very variable color pattern, not distinct color morphs.

Polymorphism

If a species of animal has different "morphs," or forms, the species is described as being "polymorphic." The differences between morphs are quite small, such as color, patterns (stripes vs. spots), or size variations. "Polymorphism" does not refer to larger differences, or changes, in body shape, nor does it refer to the tadpole and adult stages in an amphibian's life (pp. 38–41). Sometimes "polychromatism" describes species like poison-dart frogs (pp. 56–57) or African reed frogs, where outstanding variations in color or pattern are found within a single species. "Dimorphism" occurs where there are only two varieties of color or pattern.

Multiple spots forming paler yellow stripes

Skin has glands producing toxic secretions as a defense mechanism

Brightly colored parotoid gland to warn off predator

POLYMORPHIC PATTERNS
Although these fire salamanders (pp. 6–7) all have different patterns, they belong to the same species, which is said to be "polymorphic." However, because each of these salamanders lives in a separate population in different areas of Europe, each belongs to different subspecies.

Stripe instead of spots

A quartet of fire salamanders, which can be 6–12.75 in (15–32 cm) long, including tail

Protection from predators

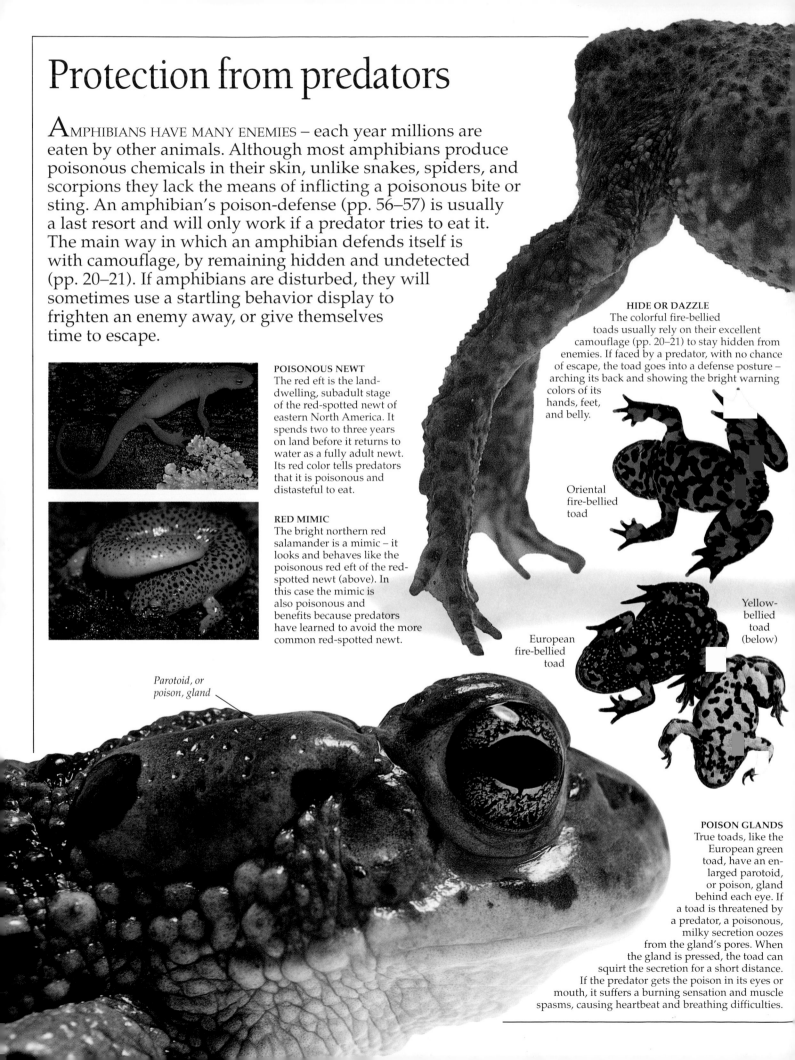

AMPHIBIANS HAVE MANY ENEMIES – each year millions are eaten by other animals. Although most amphibians produce poisonous chemicals in their skin, unlike snakes, spiders, and scorpions they lack the means of inflicting a poisonous bite or sting. An amphibian's poison-defense (pp. 56–57) is usually a last resort and will only work if a predator tries to eat it. The main way in which an amphibian defends itself is with camouflage, by remaining hidden and undetected (pp. 20–21). If amphibians are disturbed, they will sometimes use a startling behavior display to frighten an enemy away, or give themselves time to escape.

POISONOUS NEWT
The red eft is the land-dwelling, subadult stage of the red-spotted newt of eastern North America. It spends two to three years on land before it returns to water as a fully adult newt. Its red color tells predators that it is poisonous and distasteful to eat.

RED MIMIC
The bright northern red salamander is a mimic – it looks and behaves like the poisonous red eft of the red-spotted newt (above). In this case the mimic is also poisonous and benefits because predators have learned to avoid the more common red-spotted newt.

HIDE OR DAZZLE
The colorful fire-bellied toads usually rely on their excellent camouflage (pp. 20–21) to stay hidden from enemies. If faced by a predator, with no chance of escape, the toad goes into a defense posture – arching its back and showing the bright warning colors of its hands, feet, and belly.

Oriental fire-bellied toad

European fire-bellied toad

Yellow-bellied toad (below)

Parotoid, or poison, gland

POISON GLANDS
True toads, like the European green toad, have an enlarged parotoid, or poison, gland behind each eye. If a toad is threatened by a predator, a poisonous, milky secretion oozes from the gland's pores. When the gland is pressed, the toad can squirt the secretion for a short distance. If the predator gets the poison in its eyes or mouth, it suffers a burning sensation and muscle spasms, causing heartbeat and breathing difficulties.

Frogs and toads often inflate their lungs with air if upset or disturbed – if a threat increases they stand straight-limbed

Chilean four-eyed frog at rest

Parotoid gland

Chilean four-eyed frog when threatened

Eyespot

CALL MY BLUFF
Many amphibians defend themselves by bluffing, pretending they are different from the way they really are. This Eurasian common toad is standing on its toes, its body inflated with air, and its head and body tilted forward toward the predatory grass snake. This makes the toad appear larger than it really is. With the parotoid glands as a backup defense, this behavior turns the toad from an apparently harmless victim into what looks like an aggressive, dangerous attacker. The snake will probably slither away, leaving the toad alone.

SUDDEN SHOCK
The Chilean four-eyed frog has a pair of glandular eyespot markings on its flanks, which are usually covered by the thighs when the frog is at rest. If the frog is threatened, it will suddenly expose the eyespots – enough to startle almost any enemy. The "eyespot surprise" bluff is backed up by a foul-tasting poison secreted from the glands.

PRICKLY CUSTOMER
The sharp-ribbed newt has needle-like rib tips, which can actually pass through pores in the skin of its body wall. This teaches any would-be predator a sharp lesson.

Sharp rib tip

RAGING BULLFROG
This Budgett's frog from Argentina may look harmless, even funny (top), but an angry Budgett's frog (left) can look quite frightening. If this frog is threatened or provoked, it will open its mouth, scream, make loud grunting noises, and may even bite its enemy.

STRANGE POSITION
The Italian spectacled salamander uses two displays to avoid its enemies. It either plays dead or curls its tail forward to show the bright red underside of its tail (above). Many other salamander species adopt even more unusual body postures for defense. These are usually backed up by oozing poisonous or foul-tasting secretions from glands on the skin's surface.

Fast food

M OST AMPHIBIANS WILL EAT ALMOST ANY live food that they can manage to gulp down. Insects, spiders, snails, slugs, and earthworms form the main part of the diet for most adult amphibians. Larger species, like the ornate horned frog, will take larger prey, maybe even a mouse. Some species are cannibals – cases of frog eat frog. There are also specialist feeders – some smaller frogs and toads eat only ants or termites, and one species of Brazilian tree frog eats only berries. Aquatic amphibians, like the African clawed toad (pp. 22–23), tend to hang just below the water's surface, waiting for tadpoles or small fish to swim by. All amphibians will gorge themselves if food is plentiful, to enable them to survive times when food is scarce.

SNACK ATTACK
Birds, fish, insects, spiders, mammals, and even other amphibians snack on amphibians! This French earthenware plate, c. 1560, shows a frog about to be eaten by one of its main enemies– a grass snake.

Frog launching itself toward prey

1 LEAP AND SNAP FEEDING
Frogs are more active feeders than toads and will not often sit and wait for their prey – "see-it-and-seize-it" is their strategy. Launching itself toward a wood louse, this frog has to judge with split-second accuracy the distance it needs to jump and when to open its mouth.

Wood louse

2 READY FOR PREY
As the frog leaps and its mouth opens, its long, sticky tongue comes out to catch the wood louse. Frogs usually go after fast-moving insects – like flies, crickets, and grasshoppers. The frog only gets one chance – if it misses it will have wasted its energy. Even the slow-moving wood louse might fall, or get knocked off its leaf, and escape, if the frog mistimes its jump.

European common frog going after prey

Legs and body at full stretch

Eyes still open

A BIG MOUTHFUL . . .
The ornate horned frog's huge mouth, camouflaged body markings, and sit-and-wait feeding method help it take large, passing insects, mice, and other amphibians by surprise. When a horned frog opens its mouth, the whole front end of its body seems to open up!

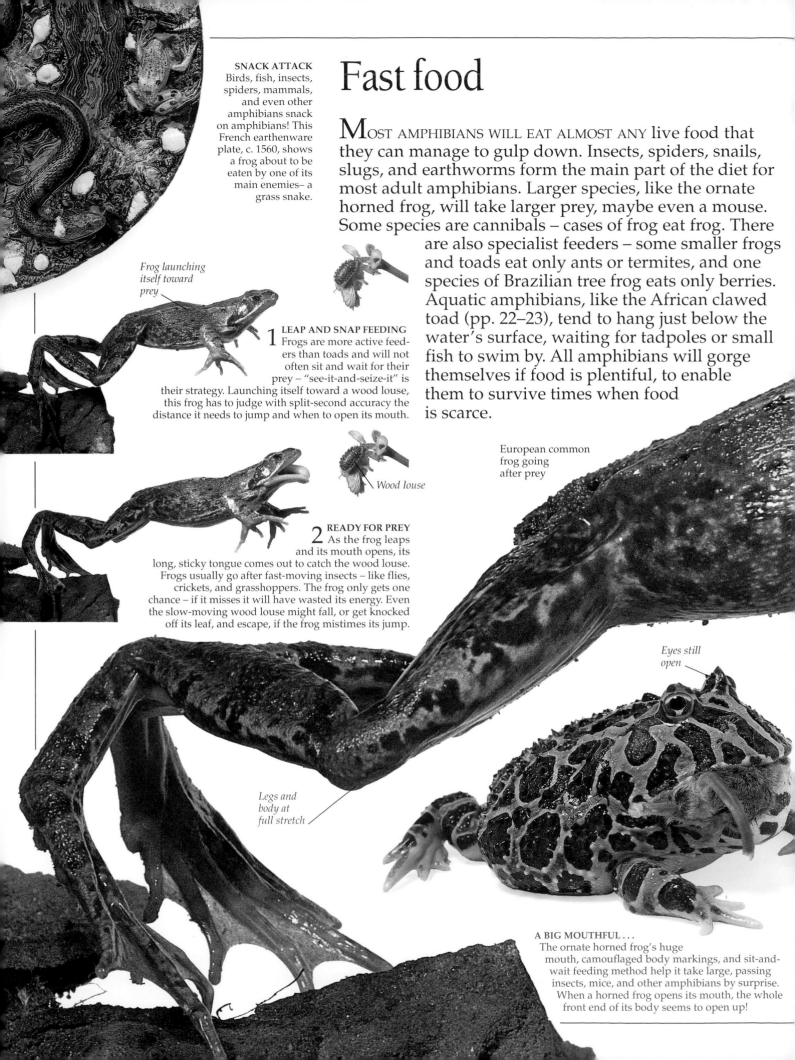

SLOW, SLOW, QUICK . . .
Newts, salamanders, and caecilians tend to eat slow-moving, soft-bodied animals, like this earthworm. They approach their prey slowly, then make a quick, last-minute grab, often turning their head to one side. They grip the food using teeth in their upper and lower jaws.

Eyelid starting to close

Wood louse

Orange striped newt eating an earthworm

Tongue flips out from front of mouth

3 SUCCESSFUL STRIKE
With the precision of a guided missile homing in on its target, the frog's tongue flips out of the open mouth and strikes the wood louse.

Making a meal of a mealworm

Watching its prey

TONGUE FLIPS
The boy's party whistle flips open and forward because air is blown into it. But the tongue of a frog or toad flips out and over, because muscles in the floor of the mouth push the tongue forward.

SEE IT, WATCH IT, EAT IT
Toads are careful, deliberate feeders. This Eurasian common toad's attention has been attracted by a wriggling mealworm. It turns its head toward its prey, watching it intently. Some toads may even stalk their prey using creeping, catlike movements. Suddenly, leaning over the mealworm, the toad gives a rapid tongue-flick, and the mealworm disappears. As the toad swallows, it blinks and the pressure of the eyeball helps push the food down.

Ready for action

Eyes firmly shut as ornate horned frog swallows its prey

Tongue flicks out

. . . TAKES SOME SWALLOWING
The blinking of the eye pushes the eyeball down, increases the pressure in the mouth, and helps the toad swallow its meal.

All but the tail has disappeared

. . . and mealworm disappears

Toad swallows, blinking its eyes

Two green tree frogs

Hide and seek

AMPHIBIANS ARE MASTERS of "camouflage" – the art of self-concealment. They have exceptional ability to use their skin colors and markings (pp. 14–15) to hide or blend in with their natural surroundings. This ability helps amphibians to avoid being seen, either by potential prey or by predators. Some species have skin flaps or fringes along the edges of their bodies; these help to make the body's outline look like a natural object in the environment, and make it even more difficult for predators to spot them. Some amphibians can remain motionless for extended periods of time, which better enables them to "melt" into the background.

HIDING IN TREES
For many species of tree frogs (pp. 50–53), being just the right shade of green is camouflage enough. Light stripes on their sides or yellow spots can look like sunlight on a leaf.

UNUSUAL STRATEGY
This tree frog from Brazil has a very unusual form of camouflage – it looks like a splash of bird droppings on a stone.

BREAKING UP
Many amphibians have a light line down their back or sides, breaking up the easily recognizable body shape. In some species, like this Gray's stream frog, the stripe may be quite wide.

LEAF MIMIC
This Asian horned toad provides one of the finest examples of the art of camouflage in amphibians. The body is flat and its color matches the dried leaves and leaf litter on the forest floor. Skin flaps, or "horns," projecting over its eyes and on the tip of its snout look like leaves, and the narrow skin ridges and glandular folds resemble leaf ribs.

PATTERN PERCEPTION
Finding a panther toad against any similarly colored background is very difficult. When the match is this good (right), and the toad remains perfectly still, it is almost impossible to see.

Asian horned toad on leaves

Panther toad on bark

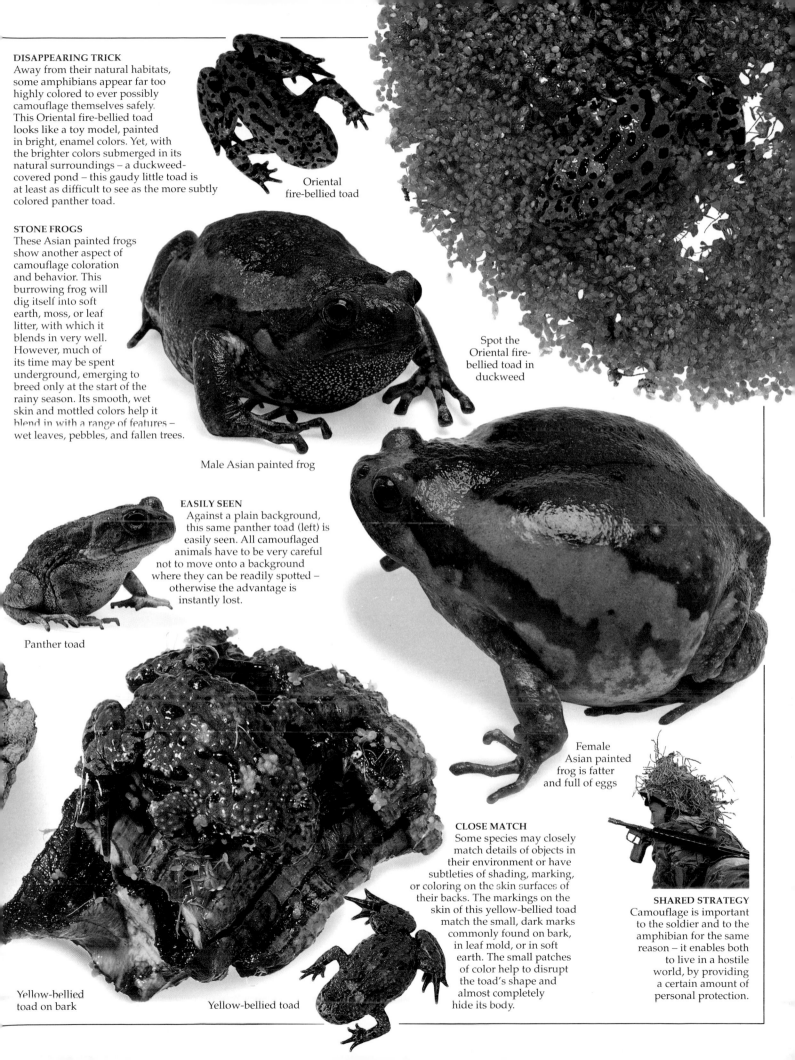

DISAPPEARING TRICK
Away from their natural habitats, some amphibians appear far too highly colored to ever possibly camouflage themselves safely. This Oriental fire-bellied toad looks like a toy model, painted in bright, enamel colors. Yet, with the brighter colors submerged in its natural surroundings – a duckweed-covered pond – this gaudy little toad is at least as difficult to see as the more subtly colored panther toad.

Oriental fire-bellied toad

Spot the Oriental fire-bellied toad in duckweed

STONE FROGS
These Asian painted frogs show another aspect of camouflage coloration and behavior. This burrowing frog will dig itself into soft earth, moss, or leaf litter, with which it blends in very well. However, much of its time may be spent underground, emerging to breed only at the start of the rainy season. Its smooth, wet skin and mottled colors help it blend in with a range of features – wet leaves, pebbles, and fallen trees.

Male Asian painted frog

EASILY SEEN
Against a plain background, this same panther toad (left) is easily seen. All camouflaged animals have to be very careful not to move onto a background where they can be readily spotted – otherwise the advantage is instantly lost.

Panther toad

Female Asian painted frog is fatter and full of eggs

CLOSE MATCH
Some species may closely match details of objects in their environment or have subtleties of shading, marking, or coloring on the skin surfaces of their backs. The markings on the skin of this yellow-bellied toad match the small, dark marks commonly found on bark, in leaf mold, or in soft earth. The small patches of color help to disrupt the toad's shape and almost completely hide its body.

SHARED STRATEGY
Camouflage is important to the soldier and to the amphibian for the same reason – it enables both to live in a hostile world, by providing a certain amount of personal protection.

Yellow-bellied toad on bark

Yellow-bellied toad

NO ROAD SENSE
Every year thousands of amphibians are killed on the roads during their annual migrations to and from their breeding ponds. Road signs like this (right) warn motorists about migrating frogs and toads.

LIKE OTHER ANIMALS, AMPHIBIANS HAVE five basic senses – touch, taste, sight, hearing, and smell. But they can also detect ultraviolet and infrared light and the Earth's magnetic field. Through touch, amphibians can feel temperature and pain, and respond to irritants, such as acids in the environment. As cold-blooded animals with porous skin, amphibians need to respond quickly to any external changes. In terrestrial (land-based) species, a sudden change in temperature can lead to death by drying out or from freezing by rapid chilling. An amphibian's senses can also help it obtain food, find a mate, and avoid being eaten.

Tentacle

MYSTERY SENSE ORGAN
Caecilians have a small tentacle extending from the eye socket or below each eye. Its function is unknown; it may be touch (picking up vibrations) or smell (helping to detect food, predators, or a mate).

FEELING THE PRESSURE
Aquatic frogs have a lateral line sensory system for detecting pressure changes from moving or stationary objects in the water. The individual lateral line sense organs, called "plaques," are easily seen on the head and along the sides of the body on this African clawed toad.

Lateral line, or plaque

Lateral line

Eye of orange striped newt (below)

Eye of marbled newt (below)

SIGHT AND SMELL
Terrestrial species, like the orange striped newt (top left), need good eyesight to spot slow-moving prey in poor light, while marbled newts (below left) use sight and smell to find food. Like most newts, they react more strongly to food in water, showing that the sense of smell is more useful in an aquatic environment.

TADPOLES TOO
Lateral line systems are also found in aquatic newts, salamanders, sirens, and amphibian larvae, like this American bullfrog tadpole. Their position and development vary in different species.

DELICATE FINGERS
Surinam toads from eastern and northern parts of
South America spend their entire lives in water.
They have long, thin, tubular fingers, which
they use for catching and manipulating prey
toward the mouth when feeding. The tips
of the fingers are star-shaped and have a
cluster of smooth, fine filaments arranged
in branched pairs. The fingers themselves
are covered in tiny spines which help the
adult to grip slimy prey, like fish. The star-
shaped tips are only fully developed in adults
and are different in related species.

(1) Vertical pupil of
red-eyed tree frog

TEMPERATURE CONTROL
Amphibians rapidly lose body water by
evaporation in hot or dry conditions.
They can sense temperature levels and
sudden dryness through their skin,
and they control their body temperature by basking in the sun if too
cold or retreating into the shade if
too hot. This painted reed frog from
South Africa is reducing the area of
its body surface exposed to the sun
by tucking in its front and hind legs.

(2) Heart-shaped pupil of
Oriental fire-bellied toad

PERFECT PUPILS
Eye color and pupil shape are very
variable in frogs: (1) vertical, catlike for night vision or
quick response to rapidly changing light conditions;
(2) heart-shaped; (3) horizontal, the more
common pupil for normal daylight vision;
and (4) round – newts and salamanders also
have round pupils.

(3) Horizontal pupil
of Asian tree toad

*Ear of
American
bullfrog*

(4) Round pupil
of Madagascan
tomato frog

BIG EARS
Hearing is one of
the most important
senses in frogs. The size
of and distance between the
ears are related to the wave-
length and frequency of the
sound of the male's call.

THE SWEET SMELL OF LOVE
Newts have an elaborate courtship
behavior, during which the male
releases chemicals called "pheromones"
from the bulbous cloacal gland at
the base of his tail. He uses his
tail to waft these secretions
toward the female.

23

Leaps and bounds

Think of frogs and you can imagine them effortlessly leaping every which way. But not all frogs can leap – some walk, crawl, run, or hop short distances. Certain tree frogs can even "fly," or glide, from tree to tree (pp. 50–51). Almost all tree frogs have sticky, sucker-like disks, or pads, on their hands and feet for clinging onto vegetation. The way frogs move is partly related to the length of their legs; short-legged frogs walk, crawl, or make short hops; long-legged frogs leap or make extended hops. A frog's behavior also affects the way it moves. It may walk slowly, stalking insects, or leap away in alarm from enemies. For any frog, the best method of escape is to make for the nearest cover, preferably by a quick leap into water. Their active lifestyle and the ability to take fast-moving prey have helped make frogs and toads the most successful group of modern amphibians, in terms of variety and numbers of species (pp. 42–45).

SERIOUS FUN
These children are having great fun playing leapfrog, but for real frogs leaping has a serious purpose. They leap so they can capture their food or escape from danger.

Leg stretching to full length

Eye closing for protection

Hump still visible

ONE, TWO, THREE, JUMP!
This northern leopard frog is showing how a long, graceful leap is made. When a frog is at rest on the ground, it sits with its legs folded. Once the frog is ready to leap, its powerful hind leg muscles and its specially modified heel section just above the feet (pp. 10–11) are put into action. Immediately before the leap begins, the frog tenses its leg muscles and then pushes its feet against the ground. The frog's leap has begun.

Northern leopard frog prepares for takeoff

Right hind leg preparing to step forward

Foot pushing against ground

Leg muscles tensing

Front leg carried down and backward

Male green toad (2.5 in, 6.5 cm long) starts a walk

RUN, DON'T WALK
Senegal running frogs (pp. 44–45) live among hummocks, or mounds, in grassland areas – a habitat where a jumping frog might become tangled in the grass stems or leap into the path of a predator. Walking or running with the body raised off the ground to clear obstacles is less dangerous.

Senegal running frog (1.2 in, 3 cm long) in crouching position and ready for takeoff

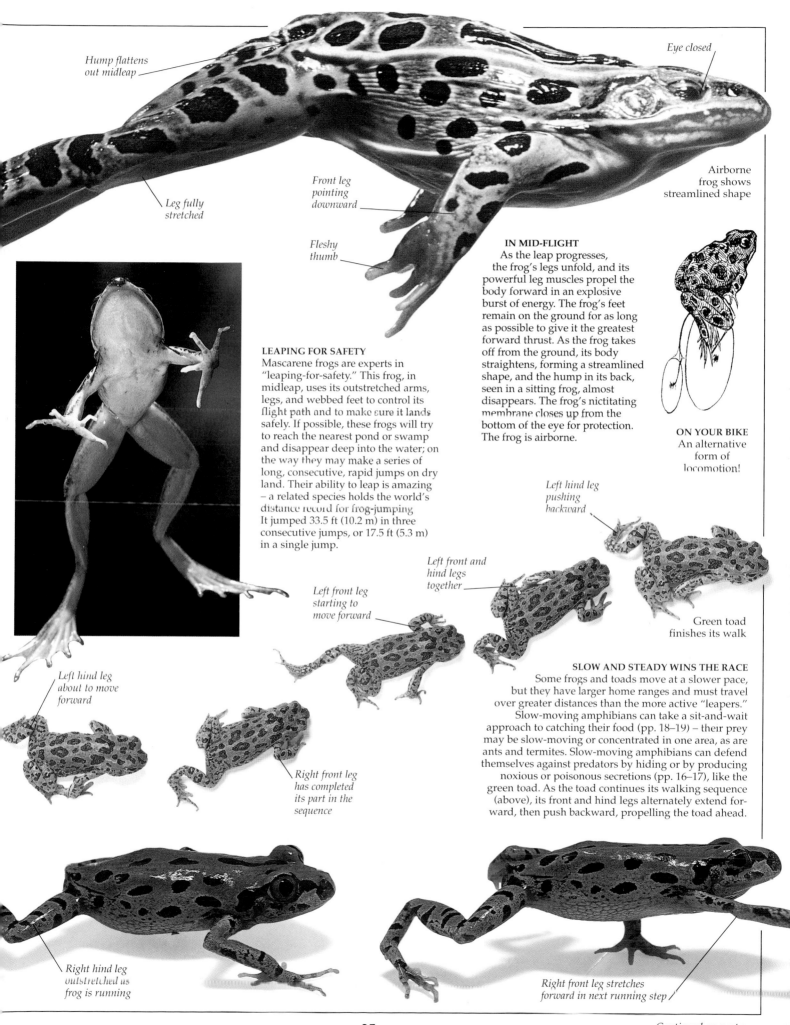

Hump flattens out midleap

Eye closed

Leg fully stretched

Front leg pointing downward

Airborne frog shows streamlined shape

Fleshy thumb

IN MID-FLIGHT

As the leap progresses, the frog's legs unfold, and its powerful leg muscles propel the body forward in an explosive burst of energy. The frog's feet remain on the ground for as long as possible to give it the greatest forward thrust. As the frog takes off from the ground, its body straightens, forming a streamlined shape, and the hump in its back, seen in a sitting frog, almost disappears. The frog's nictitating membrane closes up from the bottom of the eye for protection. The frog is airborne.

ON YOUR BIKE
An alternative form of locomotion!

LEAPING FOR SAFETY

Mascarene frogs are experts in "leaping-for-safety." This frog, in midleap, uses its outstretched arms, legs, and webbed feet to control its flight path and to make sure it lands safely. If possible, these frogs will try to reach the nearest pond or swamp and disappear deep into the water; on the way they may make a series of long, consecutive, rapid jumps on dry land. Their ability to leap is amazing – a related species holds the world's distance record for frog-jumping It jumped 33.5 ft (10.2 m) in three consecutive jumps, or 17.5 ft (5.3 m) in a single jump.

Left hind leg pushing backward

Left front and hind legs together

Left front leg starting to move forward

Green toad finishes its walk

Left hind leg about to move forward

SLOW AND STEADY WINS THE RACE

Some frogs and toads move at a slower pace, but they have larger home ranges and must travel over greater distances than the more active "leapers." Slow-moving amphibians can take a sit-and-wait approach to catching their food (pp. 18–19) – their prey may be slow-moving or concentrated in one area, as are ants and termites. Slow-moving amphibians can defend themselves against predators by hiding or by producing noxious or poisonous secretions (pp. 16–17), like the green toad. As the toad continues its walking sequence (above), its front and hind legs alternately extend forward, then push backward, propelling the toad ahead.

Right front leg has completed its part in the sequence

Right hind leg outstretched as frog is running

Right front leg stretches forward in next running step

Continued on next page

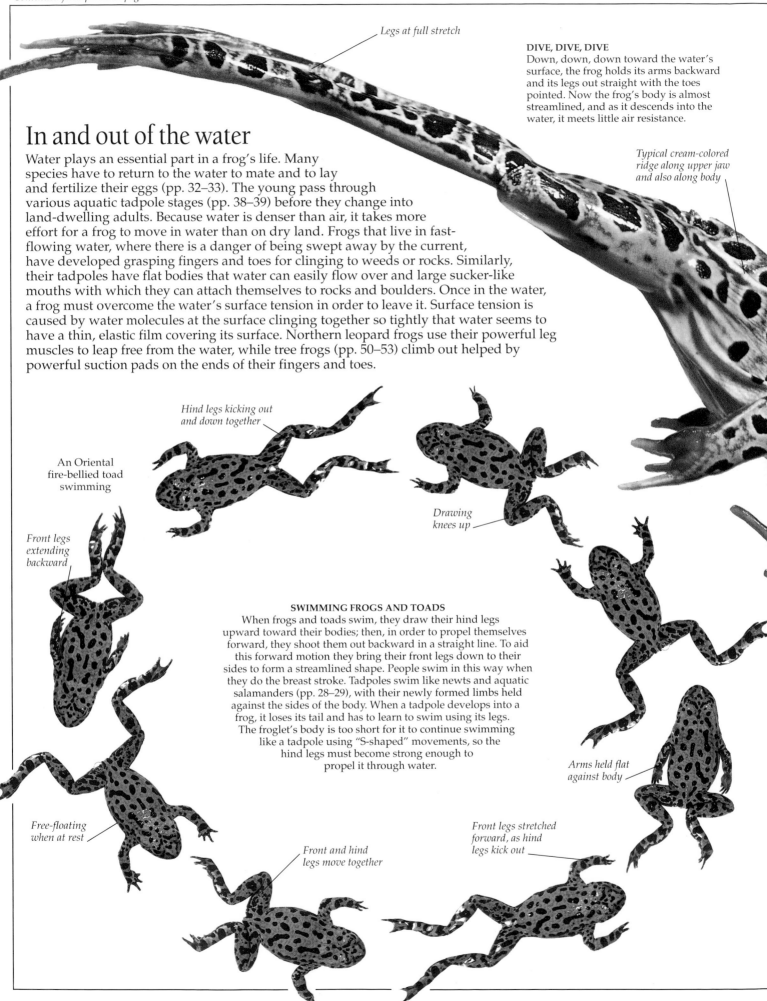

Legs at full stretch

DIVE, DIVE, DIVE
Down, down, down toward the water's surface, the frog holds its arms backward and its legs out straight with the toes pointed. Now the frog's body is almost streamlined, and as it descends into the water, it meets little air resistance.

Typical cream-colored ridge along upper jaw and also along body

In and out of the water

Water plays an essential part in a frog's life. Many species have to return to the water to mate and to lay and fertilize their eggs (pp. 32–33). The young pass through various aquatic tadpole stages (pp. 38–39) before they change into land-dwelling adults. Because water is denser than air, it takes more effort for a frog to move in water than on dry land. Frogs that live in fast-flowing water, where there is a danger of being swept away by the current, have developed grasping fingers and toes for clinging to weeds or rocks. Similarly, their tadpoles have flat bodies that water can easily flow over and large sucker-like mouths with which they can attach themselves to rocks and boulders. Once in the water, a frog must overcome the water's surface tension in order to leave it. Surface tension is caused by water molecules at the surface clinging together so tightly that water seems to have a thin, elastic film covering its surface. Northern leopard frogs use their powerful leg muscles to leap free from the water, while tree frogs (pp. 50–53) climb out helped by powerful suction pads on the ends of their fingers and toes.

Hind legs kicking out and down together

An Oriental fire-bellied toad swimming

Front legs extending backward

Drawing knees up

SWIMMING FROGS AND TOADS
When frogs and toads swim, they draw their hind legs upward toward their bodies; then, in order to propel themselves forward, they shoot them out backward in a straight line. To aid this forward motion they bring their front legs down to their sides to form a streamlined shape. People swim in this way when they do the breast stroke. Tadpoles swim like newts and aquatic salamanders (pp. 28–29), with their newly formed limbs held against the sides of the body. When a tadpole develops into a frog, it loses its tail and has to learn to swim using its legs. The froglet's body is too short for it to continue swimming like a tadpole using "S-shaped" movements, so the hind legs must become strong enough to propel it through water.

Arms held flat against body

Free-floating when at rest

Front and hind legs move together

Front legs stretched forward, as hind legs kick out

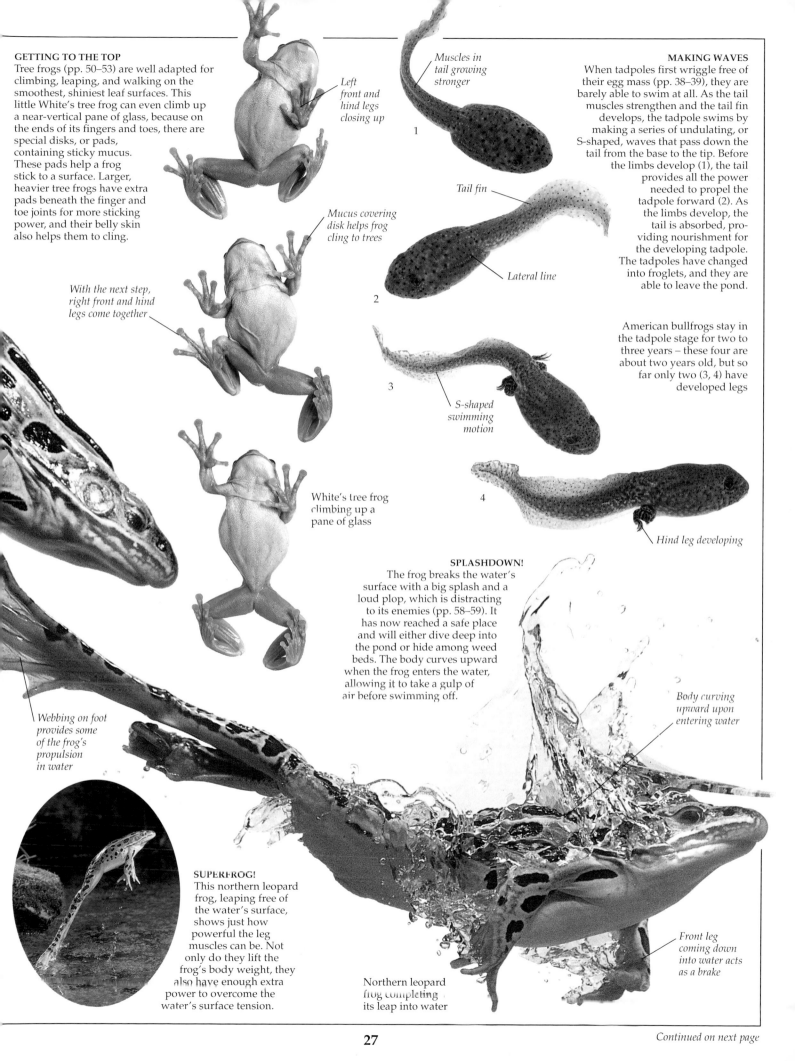

GETTING TO THE TOP

Tree frogs (pp. 50–53) are well adapted for climbing, leaping, and walking on the smoothest, shiniest leaf surfaces. This little White's tree frog can even climb up a near-vertical pane of glass, because on the ends of its fingers and toes, there are special disks, or pads, containing sticky mucus. These pads help a frog stick to a surface. Larger, heavier tree frogs have extra pads beneath the finger and toe joints for more sticking power, and their belly skin also helps them to cling.

Left front and hind legs closing up

With the next step, right front and hind legs come together

Mucus covering disk helps frog cling to trees

White's tree frog climbing up a pane of glass

Muscles in tail growing stronger

1

Tail fin

2

Lateral line

3

S-shaped swimming motion

4

Hind leg developing

MAKING WAVES

When tadpoles first wriggle free of their egg mass (pp. 38–39), they are barely able to swim at all. As the tail muscles strengthen and the tail fin develops, the tadpole swims by making a series of undulating, or S-shaped, waves that pass down the tail from the base to the tip. Before the limbs develop (1), the tail provides all the power needed to propel the tadpole forward (2). As the limbs develop, the tail is absorbed, providing nourishment for the developing tadpole. The tadpoles have changed into froglets, and they are able to leave the pond.

American bullfrogs stay in the tadpole stage for two to three years – these four are about two years old, but so far only two (3, 4) have developed legs

SPLASHDOWN!

The frog breaks the water's surface with a big splash and a loud plop, which is distracting to its enemies (pp. 58–59). It has now reached a safe place and will either dive deep into the pond or hide among weed beds. The body curves upward when the frog enters the water, allowing it to take a gulp of air before swimming off.

Body curving upward upon entering water

Webbing on foot provides some of the frog's propulsion in water

SUPERFROG!

This northern leopard frog, leaping free of the water's surface, shows just how powerful the leg muscles can be. Not only do they lift the frog's body weight, they also have enough extra power to overcome the water's surface tension.

Northern leopard frog completing its leap into water

Front leg coming down into water acts as a brake

27

Continued on next page

On all fours

Newts and salamanders (pp. 46–49) usually move quite slowly. They walk or crawl on land, underground, in the trees, or on the bottom of ponds. But they will move quickly to escape danger. Certain species can also swim or burrow: mole and tiger salamanders burrow with their hands and feet, and male aquatic newts perform swimming courtship displays in front of the females (pp. 34–35). Some salamanders live among grasses, on low bushes, and even high up in the trees; they have stubby, webbed feet for gripping leaves. So far, no "flying" salamanders have been found, but some "spring" when startled. Most of the legless caecilians are burrowers, but one group lives in water.

Tail curving to left

Foot in forward position ready for next step

Japanese fire-bellied newt swimming

SWIMMING NEWTS

Swimming involves many different leg, body, and tail movements. Newts float with their legs outstretched and body slightly inflated with air. They make slow, lazy, swimming movements using their legs like oars in a two-person rowboat. To move faster they paddle using only the front legs, only the hind legs, or sometimes alternately and sometimes together. When it needs to move quickly – for example, to escape an enemy – a newt may swim by rapidly flexing its body and lashing its tail from side to side. Watching newts swim tells a great deal about what they are doing and how they behave in different situations.

Tail is straight

Foot presses against ground pushing salamander's body forward

Foot pushes body forward

Fire salamander walking

Tail curves to right, helping salamander's balance

Foot in forward position ready to press against the ground and push the animal forward

Foot moves forward

This foot pushes the body forward

1 ONWARD AND UPWARD

The fire salamander walks slowly like most salamanders. The legs move in an alternate and opposite pattern, which means that the salamander lifts and moves the front foot of one side of its body forward at the same time as the hind foot of the other side of its body. The other two feet remain in the same position on the ground pushing the body forward, ready for the next step.

Foot ready to lift for next step

Foot in forward position ready to push body forward

Foot about to lift and move forward

Foot in forward position ready to push body forward

3 FORWARD MARCH
The third step completes the sequence, with the front left and right hind feet moving together. In addition to pushing the salamander forward, this alternate and opposite walking pattern pushes the middle of its body from side to side. This swaying motion, which increases with the walking speed, looks just like a baby crawling.

Foot ready to lift and move forward

UNDULATING CAECILIANS
Most caecilians live in soft earth or in the leaf litter of the tropical rain forest floor. About 20 species live in water and swim using undulating, or wavelike, movements like the one above. All caecilians can burrow – they push their head into the soil and open up the hole with movements of the neck. Then they either "swim" forward through the soil (using undulating movements passing back along the body) or use a special, wormlike accordion movement, where the spine (pp. 10–11) folds inside the body.

Foot in forward position ready for next step

2 NEXT STEP ON
With the next step the front right and left hind feet of the salamander move together, while the other two feet remain in the same position on the ground getting ready to push the body forward.

Foot ready to lift for next step

Foot pressing down

Foot pressing on surface, ready to push body forward

Foot about to lift

Foot ready to lift and move body forward

NEWT WALK
When on land and moving at slow speed, newts walk in a similar way to salamanders. This view from beneath shows which foot is actively pressing against the surface, pushing the newt forward, and which is being lifted off the surface before being put down again. When in water, the newt is lighter and more buoyant (just as a person is in a swimming pool) and often uses just the tips of its fingers and toes to walk over the muddy bottom of its pond.

Foot pressing down

Foot ready to lift and move body forward

View from below, showing how a newt walks

Large tubercle used for digging

All fingers and toes

An amphibian's legs, hands, and feet can give valuable clues to its habits and life-style. A closer look at the front and back legs can reveal how an amphibian moves – whether by hopping, leaping, walking, running, crawling, digging, climbing, or even "flying" (pp. 50–51). Hands and feet also show where amphibians live: tree frogs have disks on their fingers and toes; "flying" frogs have disks on their fully webbed fingers and toes; aquatic frogs and toads, as well as tree-dwelling salamanders, have very broad, fully webbed feet; and burrowing frogs have short fingers on their hands and tubercles (projections of thickened skin) on their feet.

Asian painted frog

CLIMBING HAND, BURROWING FOOT
This unusual side view of an Asian painted frog shows that it is well adapted to life on the forest floor. It has large hands with long fingers and disks on the tips for climbing and two enlarged tubercles on each foot for burrowing (pp. 54–55).

"Extra" bone in each finger and toe

Paradoxical frog

MIXED-UP FROG
The South American paradoxical frog has a strange life history. Not only does the tadpole grow larger than the adult frog, but the adult's fingers and toes each have an extra bone, making the feet and hands very long.

Sticky disk for gripping onto leaves

White's tree frog

A GOOD CLIMBER
In most tree frogs (pp. 50–53), such as this White's tree frog from Australia, both the hands and feet are adapted to climbing. Their big hands and feet spread wide, so they can grip on to larger areas of leaves, twigs, and branches, and the sticky pads on their fingers and toes help them hold on.

A GREAT BURROWER
The short, stubby toes and fingers, and large, spadelike tubercles on the African bullfrog's feet are adaptations to a burrowing life (pp. 54–55). Each year it spends up to ten months underground.

African bullfrog

African clawed toad

Claw for gripping

AN UNDERWATER LIFE
The African clawed toad's narrow hands and long fingers are used to push food into the mouth. The clawed toes grip well on slimy surfaces; and the webbed feet make swimming easy in tropical African lakes.

Web for swimming

Disk forming an almost perfect circle

HOW UNUSUAL!
This duck-billed tree frog from Belize may have an unusually shaped head, but it has the typical hands and feet of a tree frog (pp. 50–53), with long fingers and toes ending in sticky disks, or pads. The unusual angle at the end of each finger and toe, above each rounded disk, is produced by cartilage. This tough, elastic material enables the last two finger bones to slide over one another. Helped by the disks, the tree frog can prolong its contact with the surface of a tree or leaf, even if it moves a hand or foot.

Unusual head shape

Small foot with short toes

Paddle-tail newt

Fully webbed foot for swimming faster

Palmate newt

Orange striped newt

Flat foot for digging

FOUR FEET
These four hind feet show the variety of shapes found in the feet of newts and salamanders. Some species – climbers and water dwellers that live on slippery surfaces, like paddle-tail newts – have small, fully webbed feet with very short toes, sometimes contained within the web. Male palmate newts have fully webbed feet (pp. 48–49). The orange striped newt and the tiger salamander have flat feet with little or no webbing for digging.

Tiger salamander

Webbing almost nonexistent

Extra cartilage helps frog cling to leaf longer

Most salamanders and newts have four fingers on their hands and five toes on their feet

Mating embraces

Frogs and toads live in an extraordinarily wide range of habitats, but whatever the nature of their home area – on land, in water, in trees, or underground – they have to find a suitable partner and the right conditions for egg laying (pp. 36–37). Meeting, courting, and mating are the three necessary steps before egg laying can take place. In most species, the males have a distinctive mating call, which attracts females of the same species, but it may also attract predators who are always interested in large gatherings of their favorite food. Courtship behavior helps to identify the partner as a member of the same species. Once a suitable spawning ground has been found, then egg laying can begin. Amplexus – the mating embrace – places the male in the right position for fertilizing the female's eggs. Fertilization usually happens as the eggs are laid.

FROG FASTENING
Frogs and toads are popular subjects for all kinds of designs, like this 19th-century Japanese ivory netsuke, used as a kimono fastening.

SINGING AND FIGHTING
Many male frogs, like the strawberry poison-dart frogs of Central America, call and defend their territory – this is known as "lekking." The male calls from a vantage point (top) and will wrestle with any intruders (above).

TOAD HUG
Eurasian common toads often begin their amplexus, or mating embrace, out of water; the larger female then carries the smaller male to the breeding pond. Egg laying and fertilization are delayed until they are in the water.

Male grasping female under her front legs

Male and female Eurasian common toads in amplexus – on land

STUCK ON YOU
This South African rain frog is not yet "glued" onto his larger female partner – when he is, his hands will be turned palms outward. The size difference and the sticky form of amplexus prevents the male from being dislodged in the underground tunnels where the female lays her eggs.

Bi-lobed vocal sac of male frog – sacs can also be single or paired

Frog calling underwater

THE TROUBLE WITH ADVERTISING

The huge, vocal sac of the tungara frog can inflate to about the same size as its body. A common species from Central and South America, the tungara frog gets its name from its call – a loud "tung" whine followed by a sharp "ara, ara." However, for any male frogs (females rarely call), advertising their presence may have its disadvantages, such as attracting predators as well as mates. Tungara frogs are sometimes eaten by certain bats (pp. 58–59), which home in on the frog's call.

Male or female tungara frogs beat mucus and water to build a foam nest to protect and surround the egg clutch

Male

Female

Male tungara frog

A TIGHT HOLD

This male European common frog is grasping his female tightly under her arms, pressing his hands against her chest – a common form of amplexus, or mating embrace. In other species, males may hold the female around the waist – in front of the back legs – or even around the head.

Nuptial pad

Male and female European common frogs in amplexus – in water

THUMB PADS

Many male frogs and toads have nuptial pads – patches of roughened skin on the thumbs to help hold onto a slippery female during mating.

SLEEPING PARTNER

When the female red-eyed tree frog nears a calling male, he climbs on her back, and she carries him to a spawning site.

Courtship displays

IN MOST NEWTS AND SALAMANDERS, courtship and mating involves a complex behavioral display by the male for the female. Not only does a male have to find a mate of the same species, but he has to guide the female over a spermatophore, or small sperm packet, which he deposits on the ground or in a pond. Fertilization is usually internal – the female picks up the sperm packet with her cloaca, or reproductive organ. In primitive salamanders, like a hellbender (pp. 48–49), the female lays her eggs first, then the male deposits his sperm over them. Caecilians have a special kind of internal fertilization in which the male inserts the end of his cloaca into that of the female.

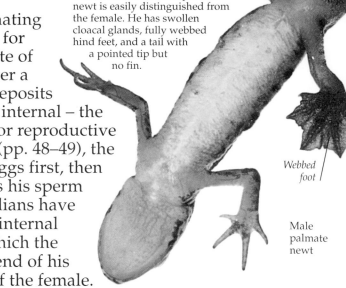

MALE PALMATE
Although he lacks the male crested newt's dramatic high-toothed crest, the male palmate newt is easily distinguished from the female. He has swollen cloacal glands, fully webbed hind feet, and a tail with a pointed tip but no fin.

Swollen cloacal gland

Webbed foot

Male palmate newt

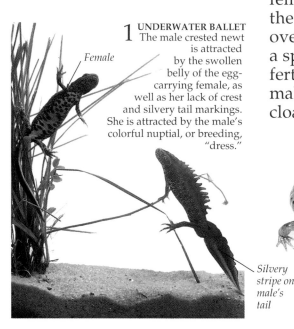

1 UNDERWATER BALLET
The male crested newt is attracted by the swollen belly of the egg-carrying female, as well as her lack of crest and silvery tail markings. She is attracted by the male's colorful nuptial, or breeding, "dress."

Female

Silvery stripe on male's tail

Male lashing tail toward female

2 DISPLAYING
The male swims in front of the female showing his breeding dress. Raising the toothed crest on his back, and lashing his silvery tail, he fans secretions from his cloacal glands toward the female.

3 NUDGING
The male deposits his spermatophore, then guides the female over it by nudging her side. The female uses her cloaca to pick up his spermatophore.

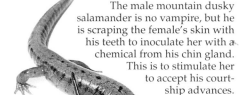

VAMPIRE SALAMANDER?
The male mountain dusky salamander is no vampire, but he is scraping the female's skin with his teeth to inoculate her with a chemical from his chin gland. This is to stimulate her to accept his court-ship advances.

FILM VAMPIRES
Hollywood vampires also use their teeth, but unlike the male salamander (top), the aim is to kill their victims.

SHOWING OFF
This 19th-century strong man shows off his strength by holding the weights with one hand, but could he hold on for 24 hours like the male sharp-ribbed newt?

MUSCULAR MALE
The male sharp-ribbed newt has well-developed, muscular forearms, an adaptation for a prolonged 24-hour mating embrace. Mating and egg laying can take place over ten months of the year, leaving out only the driest, hottest months of July and August.

Well-developed forearm for holding onto female

Normal tail – *fin extends to tip*

Thin tip to tail

THE FEMALE OF THE SPECIES
The female palmate newt lacks the male's fully webbed hind feet, swollen cloaca, and thin tip to the tail. When she is ready to breed, her belly is full of eggs. This gives her a distinctly chubby appearance, which makes the spotting on her sides visible from underneath.

No webbing on hind foot

Cloaca

Female palmate newt

Female sharp-ribbed newt

DELICATE FEMALE
The female sharp-ribbed newt's forearms are more slender than the male's. The male passes beneath the female and moves her onto his back. He uses his muscular forearms to hold onto her – they may stay in this position for 24 hours or more! He deposits a spermatophore, which she picks up with her cloaca. Then she attaches the eggs to aquatic plants.

STRONG NEWT
The male sharp-ribbed newt is either very strong or must have fatigue-free muscles to be able to keep holding onto the female for such a long time.

Pair of mating sharp-ribbed newts (female above, male below)

Male sharp-ribbed newt

Egg laying and parental care

NOT ALL AMPHIBIANS lay large numbers of eggs in water, leaving them to hatch into free-living tadpoles. Many amphibians are attentive parents and show more ways of caring for their eggs and young than fish, reptiles, mammals, or birds. The amount of parental care an amphibian gives seems to be related to the number and size of eggs produced: fewer, larger eggs receive more care; many small eggs receive less care. The kind of care ranges from choosing a sheltered egg-laying site, to enclosing the eggs in protective foam, to actually guarding the eggs. Some amphibians carry their eggs or tadpoles on their back or in a skin pocket; others take their eggs inside the body, into vocal sacs or even into the stomach; still others – two species of toads, some salamanders, and half of all species of caecilians – give birth to live young that are tiny versions of their parents.

STOMACH UPSET
This fairy tale character looks as though she is having a bad time. So are the most remarkable frogs of all – the Australian gastric brooding frogs. First discovered in 1972, they have not been seen since 1981 and may be extinct. They were the only animals in the world known to brood their young in the female's stomach.

SAFETY DEPOSIT BOX
The back of this female marsupial, or pouched, frog from South America looks swollen. The male has placed a hundred or more fertilized eggs in the brood pouch on her back. After a period of incubation, the female makes her way to the water. Using the toes on her back feet, she then opens up the pouch, releasing the tadpoles into the water to complete their development.

EGG MIMIC
The patterns on the backs of these two glass frogs from the rain forests of Costa Rica, look very similar to the eggs they are guarding. The male's camouflage enables them to guard their eggs in safety for 24 hours a day. As these frogs are so well camouflaged, they can avoid predators and feed on any insects that may alight on the leaf.

A LONG WAIT
This little lungless salamander, found in Costa Rica and Panama, is a devoted parent, guarding her egg clutch for some four to five months. The guarding parent – either the male or the female – lies curled around the eggs, which it turns occasionally. This protects the eggs from both predators and fungal infection.

Male midwife toad, ranging from 1.25–2 in (3–5 cm) in length, carries a string of eggs

A SAFE PLACE
The female Surinam toad looks like dead leaves on the muddy bottom of the sluggish waters in South America where it lives. After mating, the male fertilizes the eggs released by the female, which stick onto a thick, spongy layer of skin on her back.

Skin of female Surinam toad swells up, almost completely covering her eggs

Some males take on two, or even three, egg clutches

POCKETS FULL OF TOADLETS
The eggs are placed on the female Surinam toad's back when the male and female perform an egg-laying roll, or loop movement, underwater. The pair are upside-down when the female lays about five eggs, which are fertilized and drop onto her back as the pair turns right side up in the water. In all, about 55 eggs are laid in this way. After four weeks they hatch as perfect, small toadlets.

HITCHING A LIFT
This little, nonpoisonous frog from Trinidad is related to the more brightly colored poison-dart frogs (pp. 56–57) from Central and South America. In this species, the male stays with the egg clutch. When the eggs hatch, he carries the entire tadpole brood on his back to a nearby stream, where they complete their development. In other closely related species, the female is the tadpole carrier.

VOCAL SAC BROODING
The male Darwin's frog from Chile watches over his developing clutch of eggs, and when the newly hatched tadpoles start to squirm, he takes them into his vocal sac. The tadpoles remain there, apparently receiving some form of nourishment, until they are ejected as tiny froglets.

THE MALE MIDWIFE
The male midwife toad from western Europe shows a unique form of parental care – he carries his egg string of some 35–50 eggs, wrapped around his hind legs. After the eggs are laid and fertilized, he keeps hold of the female and, moving his legs alternately back and forth through the eggs, fastens them securely around his legs. After about three weeks he takes his egg load into the water, where the tadpoles hatch and complete their development.

NOW A FROGLET
At 12 weeks, the tail has been reduced to a bud and will soon disappear. The froglets will leave the water shortly or may have already left. Every generation re-enacts the water-to-land transition that occurred in the first amphibians (pp. 8–9).

Very short tail

Metamorphosis

M ETAMORPHOSIS MEANS "change of body form and appearance." Amphibians are the only four-limbed, or land, vertebrates (animals with a back-bone) to go through a metamorphosis – that is, a change from the larval, or tadpole, state into an adult. This change is easier to see in frogs and toads than in other amphibians (pp. 40–41). Frog and toad larvae look completely different from their parents. The most notable difference is that a tadpole has an all-in-one head and body, a long tail, and no legs. Also, a tadpole must live in water to survive. The change from newly hatched tadpole to fully formed froglet takes about 12 to 16 weeks, but this time span is greatly affected by water temperature and food supply. Tadpoles found in colder regions or at high altitudes may overwinter in the tadpole state and not turn into a frog until the following spring. Not all frogs and toads have a free-living tadpole. For some, development takes place within an egg or inside the body of a parent (pp. 36–37).

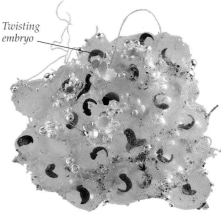

Twisting embryo

2 LIFE BEGINS
The first signs of life occur when the central yolk divides in two, then four, and then eight – until it looks like a berry inside a jelly coating. The developing embryo, or tadpole, grows longer and begins twitching. The eggs hatch about six days after fertilization.

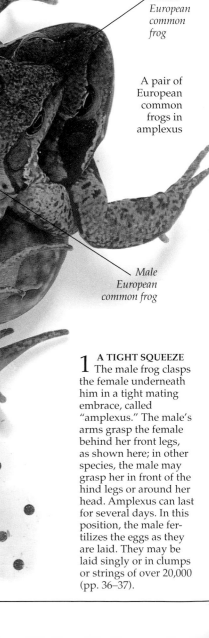

Frog's egg

Female European common frog

A pair of European common frogs in amplexus

Male European common frog

1 A TIGHT SQUEEZE
The male frog clasps the female underneath him in a tight mating embrace, called "amplexus." The male's arms grasp the female behind her front legs, as shown here; in other species, the male may grasp her in front of the hind legs or around her head. Amplexus can last for several days. In this position, the male fertilizes the eggs as they are laid. They may be laid singly or in clumps or strings of over 20,000 (pp. 36–37).

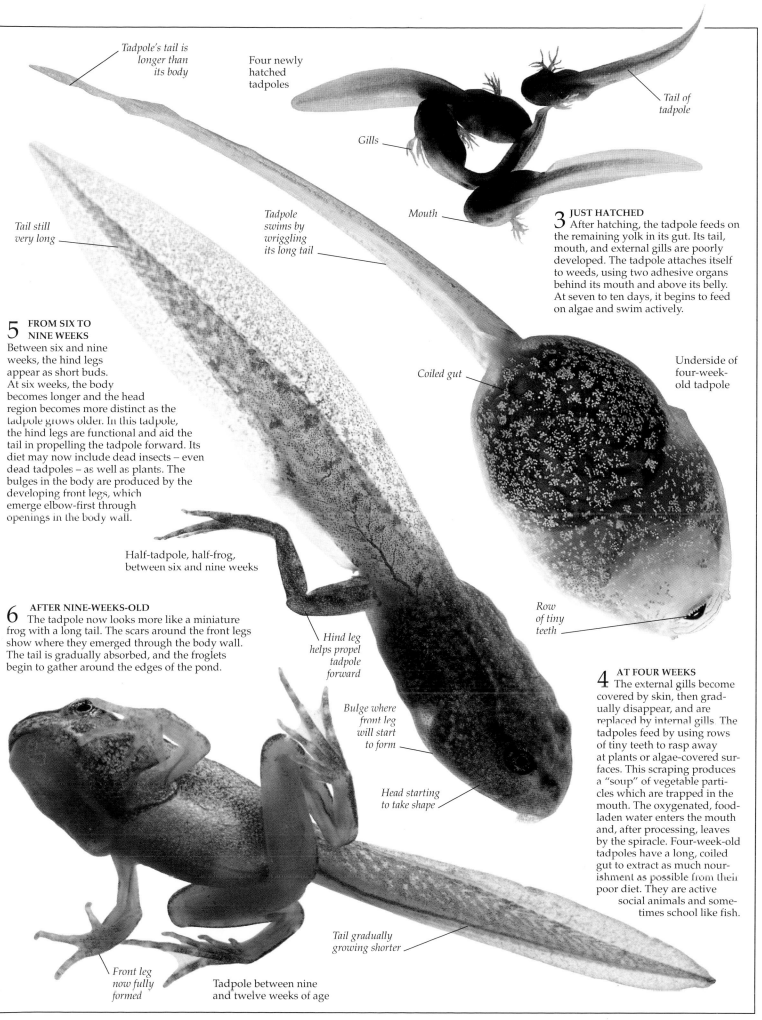

Tadpole's tail is longer than its body

Four newly hatched tadpoles

Tail of tadpole

Gills

Mouth

3 JUST HATCHED

After hatching, the tadpole feeds on the remaining yolk in its gut. Its tail, mouth, and external gills are poorly developed. The tadpole attaches itself to weeds, using two adhesive organs behind its mouth and above its belly. At seven to ten days, it begins to feed on algae and swim actively.

Tail still very long

Tadpole swims by wriggling its long tail

5 FROM SIX TO NINE WEEKS

Between six and nine weeks, the hind legs appear as short buds. At six weeks, the body becomes longer and the head region becomes more distinct as the tadpole grows older. In this tadpole, the hind legs are functional and aid the tail in propelling the tadpole forward. Its diet may now include dead insects – even dead tadpoles – as well as plants. The bulges in the body are produced by the developing front legs, which emerge elbow-first through openings in the body wall.

Coiled gut

Underside of four-week-old tadpole

Row of tiny teeth

Half-tadpole, half-frog, between six and nine weeks

6 AFTER NINE-WEEKS-OLD

The tadpole now looks more like a miniature frog with a long tail. The scars around the front legs show where they emerged through the body wall. The tail is gradually absorbed, and the froglets begin to gather around the edges of the pond.

Hind leg helps propel tadpole forward

Bulge where front leg will start to form

Head starting to take shape

4 AT FOUR WEEKS

The external gills become covered by skin, then gradually disappear, and are replaced by internal gills. The tadpoles feed by using rows of tiny teeth to rasp away at plants or algae-covered surfaces. This scraping produces a "soup" of vegetable particles which are trapped in the mouth. The oxygenated, food-laden water enters the mouth and, after processing, leaves by the spiracle. Four-week-old tadpoles have a long, coiled gut to extract as much nourishment as possible from their poor diet. They are active social animals and sometimes school like fish.

Front leg now fully formed

Tadpole between nine and twelve weeks of age

Tail gradually growing shorter

Early days

LIKE FROGS AND TOADS, newts, salamanders, and caecilians undergo a metamorphosis, or period of larval development. But the change in their body shape is less marked. In newts and salamanders, the larva looks more like the adult. The development of the crested newt is typical of species with aquatic larvae. However, many salamanders do not have a free-living larval stage. Instead, the female salamander may lay her eggs on land to be guarded by either parent, or she may keep the eggs in her body (pp. 36–37). In each case, the salamander's egg and larval development is the same as that of the newt but takes place inside either the egg capsule or the female's body. In caecilians, the species with free-living larvae have large gills and, like the adults, are limbless.

Developing embryo

Female crested newt

Egg, previously wrapped in leaf that has opened, will become part of food chain

Female uses her feet to wrap newly laid egg in leaf of waterweed

Newly laid egg

EGG SANDWICH
Newts lay their eggs singly. The female immediately wraps a waterweed leaf around each egg to hide it from predators, and so it has a greater chance of hatching. This leaf has opened, exposing the white egg, which probably will be eaten by a passing fish.

1 CAREFUL MOTHERS
This female newt is using her feet to wrap waterweed carefully around every egg she lays. Egg wrapping is a simple way of protecting the eggs (pp. 36–37) and is much safer than leaving them exposed in open water. Females of some other newts (pp. 46–49) – such as those of eastern North America and the fire-bellied newts of the Far East – show this egg-wrapping behavior. They lay between 200 and 400 eggs in this way.

2 EARLY DAYS FOR A NEWT EMBRYO
At first, the egg divides like a frog's egg – into two, then four, then eight cells, and so on, until a berrylike cluster of cells forms. After a week or so, an embryo with a recognizable head, tail, and limb buds takes shape (left). Development is rapid, and the egg hatches after only about three weeks.

Feathery gill

3 NEWLY HATCHED TO EIGHT WEEKS
Newt larvae have large eyes and usually feed on water fleas and bloodworms. They have three pairs of feathery gills, unlike frog tadpoles which have only two (pp. 38–39). Also, newt larvaes' front legs develop first; frog tadpoles form their hind legs first.

Newt larva

Internal organs and gut visible through transparent skin

One of three pairs of feathery gills

Typical large eye

Eight-week-old newt larva

Long, spindly front leg

4 EIGHT WEEKS AND AFTER
The body lengthens, the tail grows stronger, and the body outline begins to take shape. The back legs are much smaller than the long, spindly front legs. As development continues, the larva's head, mouth, body, legs, and tail take on a more adult shape. Some amphibians, such as axolotls (pp. 12–13), never develop beyond the larval stage.

Smaller back leg

Young tiger salamander with few gills remaining

Remains of gills

Young tiger salamander's tail is almost same length as its body

Feathery gill

Young tiger salamander with full gills

YOUNG TIGERS
Tiger salamander larvae are large – 0.5 in (1.25 cm) long when they hatch and 4 in (10 cm) long when they develop into young adults 12 weeks later. These two young tigers show the change from a gilled larva (left) to a nearly transformed juvenile with tiny gill remnants (above). A young salamander will eat almost any food it can get into its mouth (pp. 18–19), a habit that continues during its life. This is why it is so large – up to 1.5 in (4 cm) longer than a Pacific giant salamander.

Frog or toad?

Frogs and toads are the most easily recognized amphibians because they have such a distinctive body shape. Separating this group into "frogs" and "toads" is not so easy, as the features used to distinguish between them do not apply in all cases. In general, frogs are more active, are found in or near water, and have smooth skins, long hind legs, and fully webbed feet; toads tend to be less active, prefer to live on land, and have dry, warty skins, short legs, and little or no webbing. Yet some frogs do not live near water and have little or no webbing on their feet, and some toads have a smooth skin. The word "frogs" is often used by experts, to include both frogs and toads.

Smooth skin not typical in toads

Disk on finger

Slender body

TREE TOAD
This Asian tree toad is quite froglike – it has smoother skin than most other toads and has disks on its fingers – like the banana tree frog (bottom right). However, it belongs to the same family as the common toad (top right).

TRUE FROG
The European common frog is a typical, or true, frog – it has smooth, wet skin, a slender body, long back legs, and webbed feet used for swimming. Some of these frogs stay in the water; others leave for damp, grassy areas and are rarely seen outside the breeding season, which is how they got the Latin name of *Rana temporaria*, meaning "temporary frog." *Rana* is found throughout the world, except in polar regions, but there is only one species in Australia.

Illustration by
Sir John Tenniel
(1820–1914)

ALICE AND THE FROG
In *Through the Looking Glass*, English author Lewis Carroll (1832–1898) created the character of Alice, who on her adventures meets and befriends a frog.

Long hind leg

Typical smooth, wet skin of frog

Webbing on foot

European common frog

Long leg

Smooth, wet skin

Dry, warty skin

Short leg

Frog

Toad

LOOKING FOR DIFFERENCES

The difference between the long (leaping) legs of frogs and the short (hopping or walking) legs of toads is clearly seen above, but some species of frog have short legs. Biologists have tried to find other ways of telling frogs and toads apart and were hopeful when they discovered two chest cartilages that were joined together in frogs and overlapping in toads. But in Darwin's frog these cartilages are partly joined and partly overlapping.

Parotoid gland

TRUE TOAD

The Eurasian common toad is a typical toad – it has dry, warty skin, parotoid, or poison, glands behind the eyes, a squat body, short legs for walking or hopping, and less webbing on its feet than frogs have. Toads prefer dry land but enter water in the breeding season; however, some hibernate, or overwinter, in water.

Squat body

Dry, warty skin

Eurasian common toad

Almost no webbing on foot

TREE FROG?

This little banana tree frog has overlapping chest cartilages – which normally would make it a toad – yet it has a smooth skin and a froglike appearance, so it is referred to as a frog.

Lateral line

Short leg

AFRICAN CLAWED FROG ... OR TOAD?

Some people call this a clawed frog, and others a clawed toad. It has very smooth skin, lives in water, and has fused chest cartilages, so it should be called a frog. However, scientific names are less confusing – it is known as a *Xenopus* (zen-o-puss) throughout the world.

Banana tree frog

Continued on next page

Loads of toads and frogs

There are more than 3,500 species of frog, but new species are still being discovered every year (pp. 60–61). Frogs are by far the largest and most flourishing group of modern amphibians and are found on all the world's continents, except Antarctica. Although a few species are adapted to living in cold conditions and others live in deserts, the greatest variety is found living in tropical rain forests. Frogs have a wide range of lifestyles – aquatic, terrestrial, and arboreal – that is, they live in water, on land, and in trees, respectively. Some frogs are totally aquatic, like the African clawed toad (pp. 22–23), while semi-terrestrial species live in and around ponds, lakes, fast-flowing rivers, and torrential streams. Wholly terrestrial species include burrowing frogs, like the mole frog, which cannot swim in water. The arboreal, or tree, frogs are also found in bushes, on sedges and grasses, as well as in trees. Frogs have evolved a wide range of body shapes, sizes, and colors, that enable them to survive in widely diverse habitats.

AUSTRALIAN BURROWER
Many frogs and toads burrow (pp. 54–55), but only the aptly named mole frog from Western Australia is a supreme example of adapting to life underground. A "head-first" burrower with a small head and tiny eyes, it uses its powerful, muscular front legs, broad hands, and stubby fingers to dig, in a mole-like fashion. It lives on termites and only comes to the surface to mate – when it rains.

EUROPEAN GREEN
Most tree frogs (pp. 50–53) live in South America, but this pretty little green tree frog, at 1.5–2.5 in (4–6 cm) in length, is common in most of Europe, into Africa and Asia. It lives in woods and scrubland, and only leaves its treetop life to mate in ponds during the spring.

Typical brightly colored foot

Warty, toadlike skin

AFRICAN GIANT
Adult African bullfrogs can grow to 8 in (20 cm) in length. The males can be very aggressive when defending their territories against intruders – other bull-frogs or even humans – and are capable of inflicting a nasty bite (pp. 18–19).

Related species can have much smaller horns or no horns at all

At 7.5 in (18.5 cm) long the African bullfrog is large, but the Goliath frog from West Africa is the world's biggest frog – up to 15.5 in (40 cm) long

A LEAFLIKE FROG FROM ASIA
The fleshy horns projecting over the eyes and beyond the snout make this a very effective leaf lookalike (pp. 20–21).

ASIAN ARBOREALS
The Asian tree toad, at 2–4 in (5–10 cm) long, is an unusual toad with disks on its fingers and toes. They are good climbers and live in trees and bushes near streams in the forests of Thailand, Sumatra, and Borneo (pp. 42–43).

NO ADDED COLOURS
These four, fat tomato frogs (pp. 60–61) from northwestern Madagascar really are this deep tomato-red color, and are shaped like a tomato as well.

Madagascan tomato frogs, from 2–2.75 in (5–7 cm) long

Senegal running frog

FRIENDLY FROG
The Asian painted frog from China, Indonesia, and India is an attractive species. This pattern helps it blend in with stones and rocks, which it hides under during the day (pp. 20–21). It is often found in parks and gardens near where humans live.

Smaller male

Bold markings on top side of female's body

AFRICAN RUNNER
This brightly-colored frog is well camouflaged in its natural grassland habitat; it runs rather than hops (pp. 24–25).

A DEADLY WAITING GAME
The ornate horned frog from South America spends most of its time half buried in forest leaf litter or among moss, with just the head and eyes showing. They are "sit-and-wait" feeders and will grab any passing prey – large insects, other frogs, and even small mammals (pp. 18–19).

UNINVITED GUESTS
White's tree frogs from Australia (pp. 50–51) have an even closer relationship with humans than the Asian painted frogs – they are commonly found in outdoor mailboxes, in bathrooms, and even in toilet tanks.

Almost actual size, at 1.2 in (3 cm) long

HIGH ALTITUDE LIVING
The Chilean red-spotted toad, found at heights of 13,000 ft (4,000 m) in the Andes Mountains, has had to adapt to living at high altitudes.

FIRE FROG
The West African fire frog's skin is smooth and rubbery, but toxic secretions will ooze out, if the frog is disturbed (pp. 16–17).

Only 1 in (2.5 cm) long

45

Tailed amphibians

SALAMANDERS, NEWTS, AND SIRENS make up a group of around 360 species of tailed amphibians. Most newts and salamanders are found in the cooler, temperate, forested areas of the Northern Hemisphere, but one group of lungless salamanders (pp. 48–49) extends southward to South America to include the high-altitude tropical cloud forests of Ecuador. Like frogs and toads, tailed amphibians have a wide range of lifestyles. Some live on land in damp areas, though they may enter water to breed (pp. 34–35). Some lungless salamanders even live in trees and have broad, flat, fully webbed hands and feet with no obvious fingers and toes. Others, like the olm and axolotl (pp. 12–13), spend their whole lives in water. The caecilians, around 170 species, are found only in the tropics and burrow in soft earth or mud, often near water, or they swim in rivers and streams.

HERALDIC SALAMANDER
This dragon-like salamander – a fabulous beast of heraldry and mythology – was the emblem of the French royal family in the early 1500s. In the painting in which this detail appears, *The Field of the Cloth of Gold*, the salamander looks down on a meeting between England's Henry VIII and France's François I.

Short hind leg – toes more equal in size than in frogs

ON FIRE!
The sight of bright yellow and black salamanders fleeing from piles of burning logs gave rise to the belief that they lived in fire, hence their name – fire salamanders.

Tip of crest on crested newt's tail grows only on male during mating season

Tiger salamander

Well-developed tail

Silvery stripe in tail of male

CAECILIANS – THE UNKNOWN AMPHIBIANS
Few biologists have seen a live caecilian, and many people have never even heard of this group of limbless amphibians. Caecilians vary greatly in size, from 3 in (8 cm) to 5 ft (1.5 m) in length, and have either a short tail or no tail at all. Females produce live young or guard small clutches of 30 to 60 large eggs, that hatch into adult-like, gilled larvae.

Longer body than in
frogs and toads

Skin folds (costal
grooves) – useful
when identifying
salamanders

SHY SALAMANDER

Generally, the term
"salamander" is used
to refer only to terrestrial, or
land-based, amphibians with tails,
though aquatic newts and sirens are
also members of this family. Land-dwelling
salamanders are shy creatures and live mostly in
damp areas under cover of fallen trees, logs, and rocks.
They vary in size from the tiny dwarf Mexican lungless
salamander, about 1 in (2.54 cm) long including the tail,
up to this North American tiger salamander which can
grow as long as 15.5 in (40 cm). However, aquatic
newts and salamanders, like the Japanese giant
salamander, can grow up to 5 ft (1.5 m) long.

Front legs
only present

One of four
toes on
front foot

SALAMANDER OR SIREN?

Sirens from North America (pp. 10–11) are distinct
from salamanders in that they have lungs as well
as gills and are permanent aquatic larvae – that
is, they never develop beyond the larval
stage, so they never leave
the water.

One of five toes
on hind foot

Lesser siren

Belly marking like a fingerprint
– every newt has a unique
set of spots

Cloacal gland,
at base of
male's tail

WATERY NEWTS

Newts are semiaquatic
salamanders that return
to the water in the breeding
season. They are found in
North America, Europe,
western and eastern Asia, and
Japan. The males, particularly
those of European species like
this crested newt (right), develop
a courtship "dress" in spring and
make an elaborate display to the female
(pp. 34–35). The female lacks the crest
and silvery tail stripe of the male.

Male crested newt,
viewed from underneath

Continued on next page

Newt and salamander assortment

Newts and salamanders belong to a smaller group of amphibians than frogs and toads – there are only about 360 species. Most live in cool, temperate areas of Europe, North America, China, and Japan, but one group lives in tropical parts of South America. Adapted to a variety of habitats, they climb trees and shrubs, burrow, or lead a totally aquatic existence (pp. 28–29). The largest group, about 150 species, have lost their lungs entirely and breathe through their skin and throat instead.

"EYE OF NEWT"
The three witches in Shakespeare's *Macbeth* thought this was a necessity in their brew. "Newt" comes from the Anglo-Saxon "efete," while "an ewt" became "a newt" in Middle English. Young newts are called efts in America.

Fire salamander

SLOW MOVER
Fire salamanders are stocky and heavily built. They prefer damp areas near water and hunt slow-moving prey, such as earthworms, at night.

Fire-bellied newts are found in China and Japan

NEWTS GALORE
Most newts live on land, returning to water to breed. In the breeding season, the brightly colored male develops a crest along his back and tail. Some species also have toe webs, or fringes, which are used in courtship displays to attract the female (pp. 34–35).

The crested newt is a protected species in the U.K., but it is also found in other parts of Europe

Palmate newts live in Western Europe and spend more time in water than common newts

The crest of a male Italian crested newt is larger and more distinctive than in a crested newt

The alpine newt (left) is a very pretty European species but is not confined to alpine regions

The marbled newt from France and Spain (left) sometimes interbreeds with the crested newt (above right), producing hybrids

Broad head

Tiger salamander

HEAVYWEIGHT LEAGUE
The tiger salamander lives practically everywhere from arid plains to wet meadows all over North America. It is the largest living land salamander and may reach 15.5 in (40 cm) in length. These salamanders are voracious feeders and will even eat other amphibians. Like other members of the mole salamander family, they live in burrows that either belong to other animals or that they dig for themselves.

BIG BABY
This tiger salamander larva will change into an adult when it is about 5 in (12 cm) long – unlike its relative, the axolotl, which remains and breeds in the larval state (pp. 12–13).

Orange color of bony crests on head and back extends full length of tail

Wart

ORIENTAL SALAMANDER
The orange striped or crocodile newt is found throughout India and eastern Asia. It belongs to the same family – Salamandridae – as other newts and the fire salamander.

Tiger salamander larva

Gill

Flat, V-shaped head

COMPETELY LUNGLESS
This dwarf Mexican lungless salamander is one of the smallest salamanders in the world, measuring less than 1 in (2.5 cm) in total length.

Orange striped newt

MOUNTAIN DWELLER
The mountain dusky salamander, from the northeastern U.S., is another lungless salamander. It grows up to 4.5 in (11 cm) long. They are found in cool, moist areas near streams and in forests.

Mud puppy viewed from underneath

Gill

MUD PUPPY
The North American mud puppy is a permanent neotenic (pp. 12–13) larval species that may take up to six years to reach sexual maturity. Mud puppies have large, deep red gills, four toes on each foot, and are related to the European olm.

HELLBENDERS
These strange looking salamanders live in the eastern-central U.S. and may grow to 30 in (75 cm) long. They are totally aquatic, living in fast-flowing streams and rivers, and are related to the Chinese and Japanese giant salamanders (pp. 10–11).

Hellbender

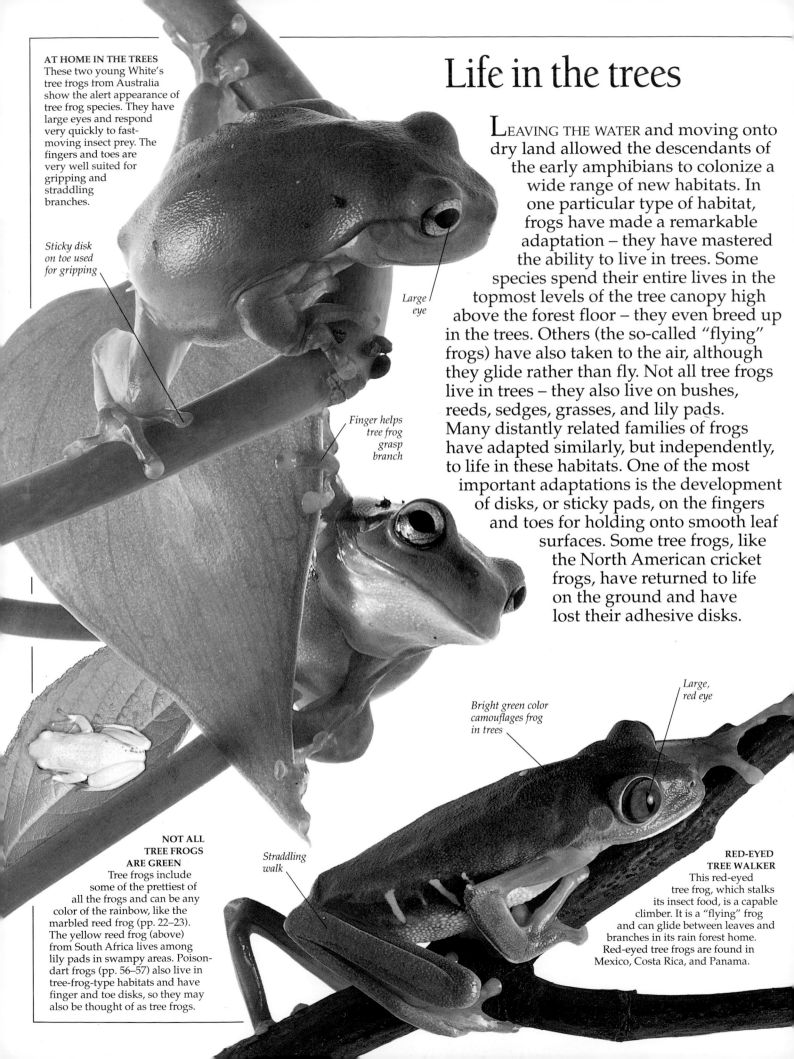

Life in the trees

AT HOME IN THE TREES
These two young White's tree frogs from Australia show the alert appearance of tree frog species. They have large eyes and respond very quickly to fast-moving insect prey. The fingers and toes are very well suited for gripping and straddling branches.

Sticky disk on toe used for gripping

Large eye

Finger helps tree frog grasp branch

LEAVING THE WATER and moving onto dry land allowed the descendants of the early amphibians to colonize a wide range of new habitats. In one particular type of habitat, frogs have made a remarkable adaptation – they have mastered the ability to live in trees. Some species spend their entire lives in the topmost levels of the tree canopy high above the forest floor – they even breed up in the trees. Others (the so-called "flying" frogs) have also taken to the air, although they glide rather than fly. Not all tree frogs live in trees – they also live on bushes, reeds, sedges, grasses, and lily pads. Many distantly related families of frogs have adapted similarly, but independently, to life in these habitats. One of the most important adaptations is the development of disks, or sticky pads, on the fingers and toes for holding onto smooth leaf surfaces. Some tree frogs, like the North American cricket frogs, have returned to life on the ground and have lost their adhesive disks.

NOT ALL TREE FROGS ARE GREEN
Tree frogs include some of the prettiest of all the frogs and can be any color of the rainbow, like the marbled reed frog (pp. 22–23). The yellow reed frog (above) from South Africa lives among lily pads in swampy areas. Poison-dart frogs (pp. 56–57) also live in tree-frog-type habitats and have finger and toe disks, so they may also be thought of as tree frogs.

Straddling walk

Bright green color camouflages frog in trees

Large, red eye

RED-EYED TREE WALKER
This red-eyed tree frog, which stalks its insect food, is a capable climber. It is a "flying" frog and can glide between leaves and branches in its rain forest home. Red-eyed tree frogs are found in Mexico, Costa Rica, and Panama.

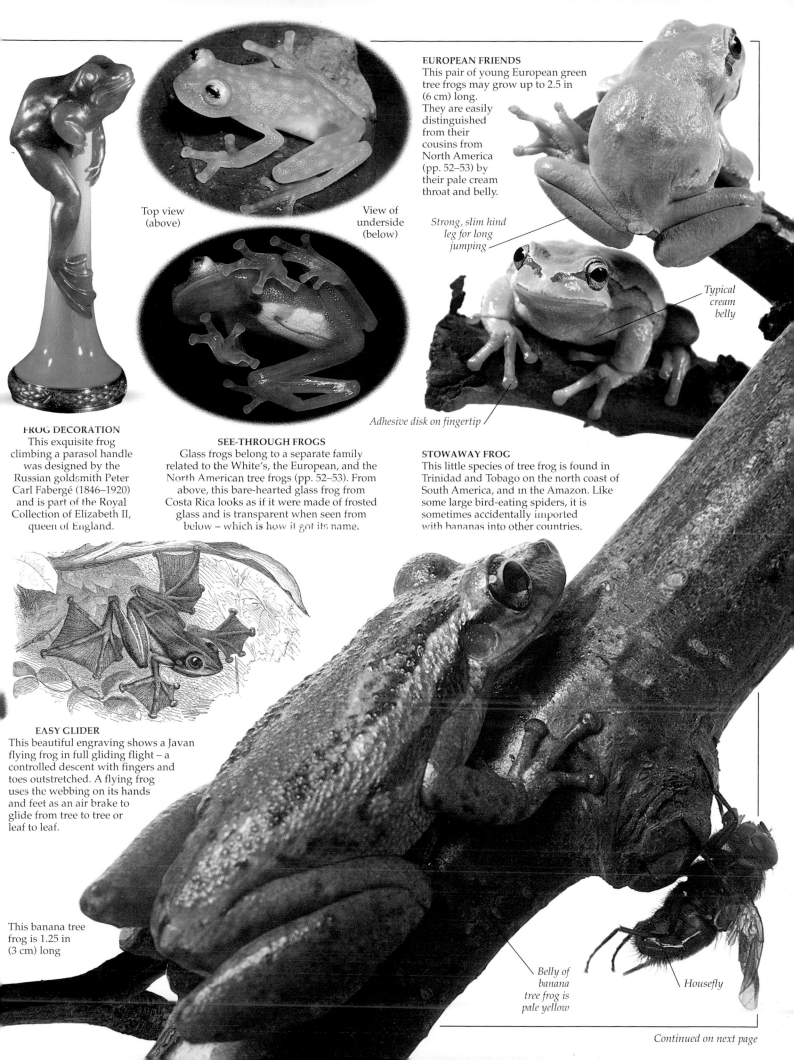

Top view
(above)

View of
underside
(below)

EUROPEAN FRIENDS
This pair of young European green tree frogs may grow up to 2.5 in (6 cm) long. They are easily distinguished from their cousins from North America (pp. 52–53) by their pale cream throat and belly.

Strong, slim hind leg for long jumping

Typical cream belly

Adhesive disk on fingertip

FROG DECORATION
This exquisite frog climbing a parasol handle was designed by the Russian goldsmith Peter Carl Fabergé (1846–1920) and is part of the Royal Collection of Elizabeth II, queen of England.

SEE-THROUGH FROGS
Glass frogs belong to a separate family related to the White's, the European, and the North American tree frogs (pp. 52–53). From above, this bare-hearted glass frog from Costa Rica looks as if it were made of frosted glass and is transparent when seen from below – which is how it got its name.

STOWAWAY FROG
This little species of tree frog is found in Trinidad and Tobago on the north coast of South America, and in the Amazon. Like some large bird-eating spiders, it is sometimes accidentally imported with bananas into other countries.

EASY GLIDER
This beautiful engraving shows a Javan flying frog in full gliding flight – a controlled descent with fingers and toes outstretched. A flying frog uses the webbing on its hands and feet as an air brake to glide from tree to tree or leaf to leaf.

This banana tree frog is 1.25 in (3 cm) long

Belly of banana tree frog is pale yellow

Housefly

Continued on next page

Male green tree frog's favorite calling site is in trees high above the ground

Bony head

Projecting bony upper lip

Sticky pad on end of finger

Cream strip from nose to tail

Head of duck-billed tree frog

GREEN SONGSTER
Tree frogs are the song-birds of the amphibian world, and their favorite calling sites are in trees high above the ground. The green tree frog has the typical tubby body shape, long hind legs, and sticky pads on the fingers and toes of a tree frog. Although many tree frogs look alike, differences in head shapes, colors, and markings are easily seen by comparing this tree frog with European and White's tree frogs (pp. 50–51).

GUESS WHO?
Kermit is probably based on the green tree frog. Male tree frogs sing to attract their females just like Kermit. But he sings his love song to Miss Piggy!

DUCK-BILLED TREE FROG
Seen from the side, the head of this tree frog from Belize has a very unusual shape. The snout's bony ridges and "duck-bill" shape make the frog's head look very similar to that of the duck in this old engraving. They also make the frog look less froglike, and the bony ridges help to camouflage it against tree bark.

A safe haven
The ancestors of modern tree frogs were probably attracted to the safety of vegetation, which was mostly free from predators, and to the more plentiful supply of insects that lived around the plants. Early tree frogs were probably better at grasping tall grasses, twigs, leaves, and leaf stems than other frogs. Many amphibians, particularly frogs and toads (pp. 8–9), migrated from life on the ground to life in the surrounding vegetation above during the course of their evolution. Many modern tree frogs are vividly colored. Seen away from their natural habitat, it is difficult to realize that their bright colors help to camouflage (pp. 20–21), as well as warn, or confuse, their enemies.

Skin's green color helps tree frog merge into background

Dark markings on frog's back match tree bark

Unusual head shape helps with camouflage

BONE HEAD

The skin on the heads of these two unusual tree frogs from Belize in Central America is fused to the bony, boxlike skull; this may help to reduce water loss (pp. 12–13). The tree frog protects itself from predators by backing into a hole in a tree trunk and using its head to block the entrance.

Bony eyebrow protects eye (smaller than in most tree frogs)

Large, sticky, rounded disk on end of finger for gripping bark

1 FROM A SAFE PLACE
Against a leafy background this red-eyed tree frog would be well hidden. The green color of its head, back, and legs, and the vertical stripes on its sides make it look like a leaf in dappled sunlight.

2 DANGER AHEAD
Jumping in trees is dangerous. A tree frog could easily hit (or miss) a branch, injure itself, or become tangled up in leaves and stems. Any movement is dangerous because it might also attract predators.

RED ALERT

This red-eyed tree frog from Central America is sitting in a typically alert tree frog posture. Tree frogs peer over the edges of leaves and branches to look out for both prey and predators, while hiding as much of themselves as possible (pp. 22–23).

Tree frog's eye typically facing forward

3 FULLY STRETCHED
The bright orange color on the thighs and other usually hidden surfaces is an example of "flash coloration." A sudden flash of color, combined with the jumping tree frog's unusual shape, confuses its enemies. When tree frogs land almost flat onto a leaf surface, they make a very quiet "slap" sound.

Flash color of bright orange (but it can also be red, blue, or yellow)

Earth movers

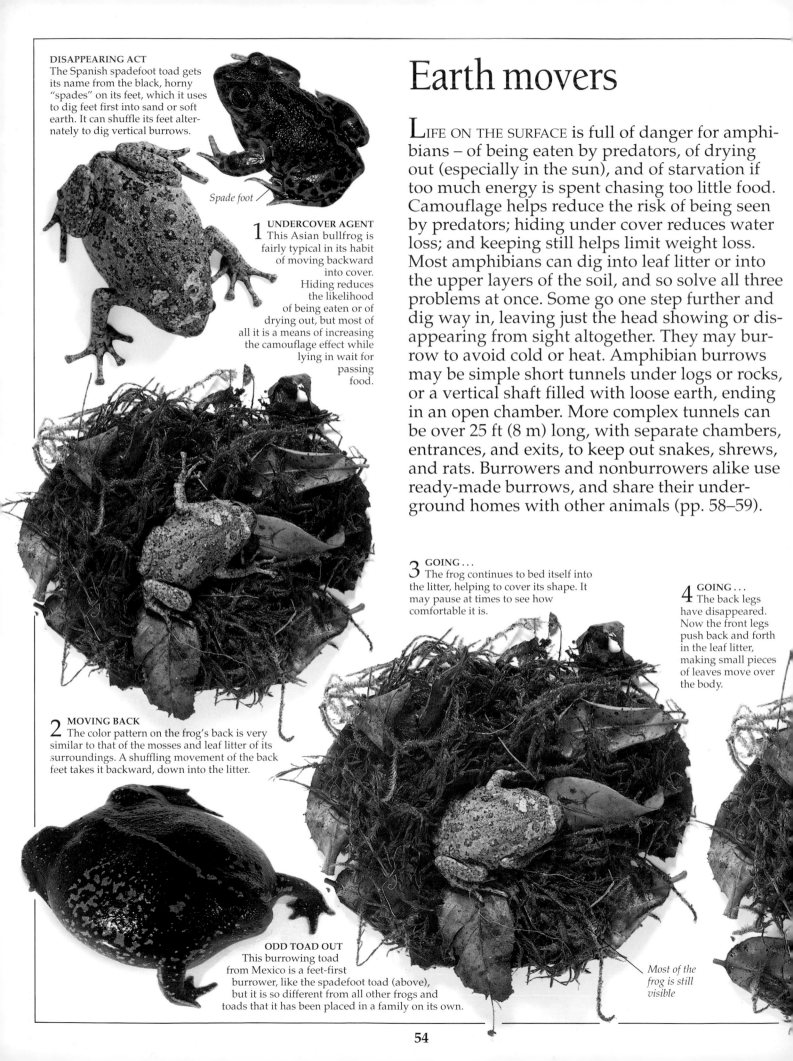

DISAPPEARING ACT
The Spanish spadefoot toad gets its name from the black, horny "spades" on its feet, which it uses to dig feet first into sand or soft earth. It can shuffle its feet alternately to dig vertical burrows.

Spade foot

1 UNDERCOVER AGENT
This Asian bullfrog is fairly typical in its habit of moving backward into cover. Hiding reduces the likelihood of being eaten or of drying out, but most of all it is a means of increasing the camouflage effect while lying in wait for passing food.

LIFE ON THE SURFACE is full of danger for amphibians – of being eaten by predators, of drying out (especially in the sun), and of starvation if too much energy is spent chasing too little food. Camouflage helps reduce the risk of being seen by predators; hiding under cover reduces water loss; and keeping still helps limit weight loss. Most amphibians can dig into leaf litter or into the upper layers of the soil, and so solve all three problems at once. Some go one step further and dig way in, leaving just the head showing or disappearing from sight altogether. They may burrow to avoid cold or heat. Amphibian burrows may be simple short tunnels under logs or rocks, or a vertical shaft filled with loose earth, ending in an open chamber. More complex tunnels can be over 25 ft (8 m) long, with separate chambers, entrances, and exits, to keep out snakes, shrews, and rats. Burrowers and nonburrowers alike use ready-made burrows, and share their underground homes with other animals (pp. 58–59).

3 GOING . . .
The frog continues to bed itself into the litter, helping to cover its shape. It may pause at times to see how comfortable it is.

4 GOING . . .
The back legs have disappeared. Now the front legs push back and forth in the leaf litter, making small pieces of leaves move over the body.

2 MOVING BACK
The color pattern on the frog's back is very similar to that of the mosses and leaf litter of its surroundings. A shuffling movement of the back feet takes it backward, down into the litter.

ODD TOAD OUT
This burrowing toad from Mexico is a feet-first burrower, like the spadefoot toad (above), but it is so different from all other frogs and toads that it has been placed in a family on its own.

Most of the frog is still visible

The South African spotted shovel-nosed frog

6 GONE
Only the head is showing. The frog has gained a major advantage by its activity – it is well concealed and comfortable. It can reduce its water loss and even take up water through its skin via contact with damp soil and leaves. By staying still, it will not lose weight by burning energy chasing food. All it has to do now is wait for its prey to walk by

HEAD FIRST
The spotted shovel-nosed frog from South Africa is a head first burrower with a difference – it actually uses its head, or rather its snout, for burrowing. The body is bent forward, head down, and the back legs held straight, pushing the frog's snout forward into the soil. Digging is done by raising and lowering the snout, scraping soil away with its powerful hands. Other head first burrowers, like midwife toads (pp. 36–37) and mole frogs (pp. 44–45), use only their hands and feet.

5 ABOUT TO GO
The legs and back half of the body are now hidden. The wriggling movements continue; the body is rotated, pushing it down into the leaf litter.

Only the frog's head is visible

Poison-dart frogs and mantellas

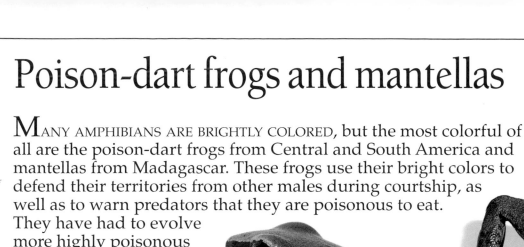

DANDY FROG
This exquisitely dressed frog, looking just like a poison-dart frog in his clothes of many colors, is all puffed up and in his Sunday best.

M ANY AMPHIBIANS ARE BRIGHTLY COLORED, but the most colorful of all are the poison-dart frogs from Central and South America and mantellas from Madagascar. These frogs use their bright colors to defend their territories from other males during courtship, as well as to warn predators that they are poisonous to eat. They have had to evolve more highly poisonous chemicals in their skin as their enemies, including snakes and spiders, become resistant to milder skin toxins.

Bright color helps to warn predators

Red flash color helps camouflage frog

This bright mantella has a red "flash" color on the inside of its leg

This yellow mantella may be a color variety of the green and black mantella (below), or a different species

STRANGE NAME
The strawberry poison-dart frog was originally given its common name because of its usual strawberry red color, made even brighter by deep blue-black flecks. But strawberry poison-dart frogs from different areas may have different colors – blue, green, yellow, orange, spotted, plain, and even black and white.

Identifying mantellas is very difficult – they have so many color varieties (above)

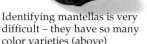

WAR PAINT
Some native peoples of North America used war paint to strike terror into the hearts of their enemies. This Hopi chief wears orange, red, and yellow – the classic warning colors – in his headdress. Amphibians also use the same colors to frighten away their enemies.

Skin is highly toxic

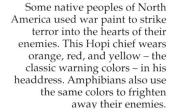

GOLDEN LOOK-ALIKE
This golden yellow poison-dart frog, *Phyllobates bicolor*, looks very much like its close relative – the more poisonous *Phyllobates terribilis* (pp. 60–61) – but it is smaller and has black markings on its legs.

It has recently been discovered that the golden mantella from Madagascar produces the same kind of chemical poisons as South American poison-dart frogs

This green mantella, first described in 1988, is from Madagascar, where habitat destruction is a problem. It is important to know about new species so they can be protected (pp. 60–61)

Bright black and red stripes make this frog more visible, to warn away enemies

FASCINATING FROGS
Poison-dart frogs make up a fascinating group. Some are brightly colored and highly poisonous, having complex chemicals in their skin. These frogs range in size from the very small (at 0.6 in, or 1.5 cm long) to larger ones (up to 2 in, 5 cm), like the two highly colored frogs sitting on the leaves (right). Poison darts are social animals, with complex territorial, courtship, and mating behaviors.

LIFE IN THE PENTHOUSE
This spotted poison-dart frog was discovered in 1984 It is found 48–65 ft (15–20 m) up in the treetops of the cloud forests of Panama. There may be many more high-level, tree-living species of amphibians waiting to be discovered.

POISONED DARTS
The Choco Indians, who live in western Colombia in South America, poison the tips of their blowpipe darts with the toxin from poison-dart frogs. They remove the toxin by heating the live frog over a campfire. Only a few species are used, but one is so poisonous (pp. 60–61) that the dart has only to be wiped against the live frog's back for it to be deadly.

Poison-dart frogs are social animals, living in small groups

HAWAIIAN HOLIDAY
This metallic green poison-dart frog from Costa Rica, Panama, and Colombia has been introduced into the islands of Hawaii and, like some of the other species, has also been bred in captivity.

When colors develop, the poison develops too

INSECT SIZE AND SOUND
One of the smallest poison-dart frogs (under 0.75 in, 2 cm), this species was discovered in 1980 in isolated patches of forests in the Andes Mountains. Its scientific name means "buzzer," after its insect-like call.

Yellow and black are warning colors, as in this poison-dart frog and in the fire salamander (pp. 14–15)

TOXIC TADPOLES
Poison-dart frogs carry their tadpoles, often one at a time, to small isolated pools, where they develop their colors and skin poisons as they grow.

Friends and enemies

AMPHIBIANS HAVE FEW FRIENDS but many natural enemies; they are eaten by a wide range of animals. To survive, most amphibians have evolved superb camouflage colors and other means of defense (pp. 16–17). They also produce large numbers of eggs, and some have special ways of caring for their young. People are the amphibians' worst enemies: we threaten their survival by polluting and destroying their habitats. Burrowing animals often help amphibians unknowingly, by providing them with ready-made burrows. Sometimes different species of amphibians will share a habitat or even burrow together. Some people are friends to amphibians and try to protect them and their environment.

THREATENED BY BATS
In tropical areas, bats have learned to home in on calling frogs, but bats do not have things all their own way. At least one species of frog from Australia is known to eat bats.

FROGS VS. MICE
Ancient Greeks used animals in their fables to poke fun at political leaders. In this 16th-century engraving of the Trojan Wars, the frog-people won the war against the mice-people when crabs pinched off the mice's legs.

A SECOND SKIN
Like other amphibians, the African dwarf clawed toad – a relative of the Surinam toad and the African clawed toad (pp. 22–23) – sheds its skin every five to seven days. This action may get rid of parasites attached to the toad's skin.

Wrinkled skin starting to lift off and shed

Webbed feet make the clawed frog a powerful swimmer

MANY ENEMIES
As shown in this print by naturalist artist John James Audubon (1785–1851), many water birds, like these black-crowned night herons, eat vast numbers of frogs. Other amphibian predators include spiders and large insects, as well as snakes, mammals, and large frogs.

DOOM
In this fable by Aesop (620–560 B.C.), a mischievous frog ties a mouse to his foot. When the frog dives into a pool, the mouse drowns. A passing hawk eats both of them – the frog becomes a victim of his own prank.

INDOOR FROG
Many frog species share human homes, especially bathrooms, like this tree frog from Southeast Asia.

BEST OF FRIENDS
In western Europe, natterjack and midwife toads (left and center in burrow) often share the same home. They may share the same burrow for their whole lives. Many other animals, like newts (right in burrow), also take advantage of the safe retreat of a ready-made burrow, with its food supply of earthworms, spiders, and beetles. The burrows may be up to 26 ft (8 m) long, with a shallow entrance 6–10 in (15–25 cm) below ground.

10½p
The Wind in the Willows
The Year of the Child

TOAD AND FRIENDS
Frogs are popular figures on stamps. Here are Mr. Toad and his friends, Mole, Rat, and Badger, from the classic children's tale, *Wind in the Willows*, by Scottish-born Kenneth Grahame (1859–1932).

Rare and endangered

Many species of amphibians are rarely seen because they are secretive, like burrowing frogs, or because their natural habitats are inaccessible. Others are seldom found outside a small geographical area. Although amphibians new to science are still being discovered at the rate of 15 to 25 species a year, many others are becoming rarer due to global warming, low water levels, pollution, acid rain, and the destruction of their habitats, such as the cutting down of rain forests or the filling in of ponds. Preserving natural habitats (pp. 62–63) is the most important step in preventing these fascinating animals from becoming extinct.

MORE PRECIOUS THAN GOLD
This 2,000-year-old Chinese gold frog is valuable, but when a species disappears, it is gone forever!

Cream throat and belly

Pair of tomato frogs from Madagascar, an island off the southeast coast of Africa

Tomato color, which can range from deep red to pale orange

THE WORLD'S MOST POISONOUS FROG
The bright yellow *Phyllobates terribilis*, first described as new to science in 1978, deserves its name. This poison-dart frog, which looks similar to *Phyllobates bicolor*, is so poisonous that it could possibly kill a person.

The poisonous *Phyllobates terribilis* was discovered in Colombia

NEVER UPSET A SKUNK!
Skunks have an unpleasant defensive behavior. If provoked, they spray a rotten-smelling liquid from glands at the base of the tail. The skunk frog (below) produces its foul smell from its skin, which exudes a thick mucus.

Skin, when touched, produces foul smell and thick mucus

Venezuela skunk frog

A BAD SMELL IN THE FOREST
The Venezuela skunk frog was described as new to science in 1991. It is the largest member of the poison-dart frog family (pp. 56–57), but its claim to fame rests on the very unpleasant odor that it gives off if it is in danger. Like its namesake (above), the skunk frog uses its odor for defense, to drive away its enemies.

DISAPPEARING NEWT
The crested newt is now on the protected species list in the U.K. – a special license is necessary even to examine it in the wild. Twenty years ago, it was abundant all over Europe, but by filling in home ponds and using agricultural poisons, people have taken their toll.

WILL THIS SALAMANDER SURVIVE?
The gold striped salamander from northern Spain and Portugal depends upon natural brooks and streams for its larval development. The removal of large amounts of water for agricultural and human use has seriously threatened its survival.

A STEP IN THE RIGHT DIRECTION
These tomato frogs (left) are endangered, like many other frog species in Madagascar, but they are listed as an Appendix I species, which means they receive the highest level of protection in law. They have, however, been successfully bred in captivity. Captive breeding and the protection of natural habitats in nature reserves may permit the reintroduction of this and other frog species back into the wild.

Crested newt's tail is almost as long as its body

AN UNREPEATABLE PHOTOGRAPH?
Gatherings like this group of male golden toads (the females are olive brown with bright red spots) in the Monteverde Cloud Forest Reserve in Costa Rica in 1985 may be a thing of the past. They have not been seen at all in this region since 1990.

ISLAND FROGS
This is Hamilton's frog, the rarest of three native species in New Zealand. It has been found only on two offshore islands in the Cook Strait. One population lives among a pile of rocks known as "Frog Bank" on Stephens Island; a second, larger population lives in a small patch of forest on Maud Island. If rats were introduced by accident, especially onto Stephens Island, this rare frog could easily be wiped out in a very short time.

Typical stunning golden color

UNDER THREAT
This golden mantella (pp. 56–57) from Madagascar is threatened by habitat destruction as are many other species of frogs (and other animals) on the island. Madagascar has a high level of "endemism" – that is, most of its species are found only there and nowhere else in the world.

Conservation

HELPING HAND
Madagascan tomato frogs are endangered. They have been bred in captivity successfully, so if wild populations become extinct, they will still survive.

THE PROBLEMS people cause by destroying habitats – for example, cutting down rain forests, filling in natural ponds, taking water from rivers for industrial use, acid rain pollution, global warming, and lowering the levels of fresh water – all threaten amphibian survival. People must change their attitude to the environment and wildlife. Like all animals, amphibians have a right to live undisturbed in their natural habitats. Conserving natural habitats and creating places for amphibians in gardens and parks will help ensure their continued survival. Studying amphibians and informing people about them help their conservation and show how important frogs, toads, newts, salamanders, and caecilians are in the beautiful natural world around us.

YOUNG NATURALIST
Caring young naturalists help to save amphibians, by raising tadpoles from frog spawn and releasing them into garden ponds.

DOING TOO WELL!
Introducing foreign species into a country can be harmful – they may compete with the native amphibians. In 1935, the marine toad was introduced into Australia to control the cane beetle infecting the sugar cane. This toad has bred so successfully that it has become a serious pest in coastal areas of Queensland and northern New South Wales.

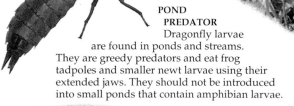

POND PREDATOR
Dragonfly larvae are found in ponds and streams. They are greedy predators and eat frog tadpoles and smaller newt larvae using their extended jaws. They should not be introduced into small ponds that contain amphibian larvae.

Frog tadpole

Pond snail keeps water free of too much algae

Newt larva feeds on water fleas

Tadpole feeding on a small piece of meat – it also eats boiled lettuce leaves

Water boatman

Newt larva develops front legs first; frogs develop hind legs first

A TANGLE OF TADPOLES
Raising tadpoles from frog spawn and seeing them transform into small adults is fascinating. Sensitive to pollution and acid rain in fresh water, tadpoles are good indicators of change in the environment.

Waterweed provides oxygen to keep pond water fresh

Fringing plants and logs provide cover for adult amphibians

RARE TOADS
The natterjack toad is a protected species in the U.K. Its continued survival depends on carefully managing its habitats.

Natterjack toad lives in heathlands and sand dunes

WATER BOATMAN
This insect swims upside down in the water, using its large, oar-like back legs, and it also eats tadpoles!

FEEDING SNAILS
Watch how snails feed, compared with tadpoles reared in a tank. They both rasp away at algae-covered surfaces and aquatic plants.

GARDEN PONDS
Garden ponds (above) are vital to the survival of amphibians. A garden pond can be made quite cheaply using a black polythene or Butyl rubber liner. The pond should have shallow and deep areas and it should be as large as possible. In the northern hemisphere the pond should be at least 2 ft (60 cm) deep, to prevent it freezing solid in winter.

Waterweed provides oxygen, food, and cover for tadpoles

Rubber liner – up to 2 ft (60 cm) deep

Index

Acknowledgments

Dorling Kindersley would like to thank:
Peter Hayman of the British Museum, Harry Taylor of the Natural History Museum, and Michael Dent (London) for additional special photography. Dr. Gerald Legg, Jeremy Adams, and John Cooper of the Booth Museum (Brighton); the British Dendrobates Group; Peter Foulsham of the British Herpetological Supply; Ken Haines; David Bird, Myles Harris, Fiona MacLean, and Robert Stephens of Poole Aquarium; Regent Reptiles; the Reptile-arium; and Roger Wilson of the Rio Bravo Field Studies Centre (Belize), for providing species information and specimens for photography. The staff of the British Museum (especially Lesley Fiton,

Catharine Harvey, Sarah Jones, Richard Parkinson, Peter Ray, and James Robinson), and the Natural History Museum (especially Ann Datta, Dr. Angela Milner, and Tim Parmenter) for their research help. Doris Dent and Alan Plank for providing props for photography. Alex and Nicola Baskerville, and Amy Clarke as photographic models. Céline Carez for research help. Manisha Patel, Sharon Spencer, and Helena Spiteri for their design and editorial assistance.
Jane Parker for the index.

Illustrations Joanna Cameron

Picture credits
t=top, b=bottom, c=center, l=left, r=right
Zdenek Berger: 8tc.
Biofotos: Heather Angel 23tl, 35br, 37tl;
Brian Rogers 37tcr.
Prof. Edmund D. Brodie Jr.: 16bcr, 17bcr, 36bc, 47cr, 49c, 49bl, 56c.
Dr. Barry Clarke: 20bcl, 23tc, 50cl.
Bruce Coleman Ltd: John Anthony 61tr; Jane Burton 16tr; Jack Dermid 16tcr, 49cb; Michael Fogden 36bcl, 37bcr, 61cr; Jeff Foott 60cr; A.J. Stevens 55tl, 55cl.
Dorling Kindersley: Frank Greenaway 38tl, 38tr, 38b, 39tr, 39cr; Colin Keates 8b, 9tc, 9tr; Dave King 11tl; Karl Shone 7tr; Kim Taylor and Jane Burton 39cl, 39b; Jerry Young 12tr, 20bl, 23tr, 30cl, 44cr, 50b.
Mary Evans: 14tl, 32tl, 36tr, 46cl, 48tr, 56tl, 57cr.
Copyright Jim Henson Productions, Inc. Kermit the Frog is a trademark of Jim Henson Productions, Inc.

All rights reserved: 52tr.
Image Bank: Al Satterwhite 21br.
Kobal Collection: 34bc.
Mike Linley: 13tr, 17bl, 17cl, 20bcl, 32tcl, 32bcl, 32cr, 32bl, 33bc, 36tcl, 54t.
Musée Nationale d'Histoire Naturelle: 8tr, 9tl.
C.W. Myers, American Museum of Natural History: 57tcl, 57cl, 60bl, 60bc.
Motoring Picture Library, National Motor Museum at Beaulieu: 6tl.
Naturhistoriska Riksmuseet: 8c.
NHPA: ANT 44tr, 61bl; Stephen Dalton 25cl, 27bl; Jany Sauvanet: 29cr, 46cb.
Oxford Scientific Films: Kathie Atkinson 13tl, 13tc; Jim Frazier 13r; Michael Fogden 22tcr, 51tc, 51c; Z. Leszczynski 7cl.
Royal Collection, St James's Palace, copyright Her Majesty the Queen: 46tr, 51tl.
Paul Verrell: 34c.
Zefa: 56cr; K. & H. Bensor 19bcl.

 AMPHIBIAN   ANCIENT CHINA  ANCIENT EGYPT  ANCIENT GREECE  ANCIENT ROME   ARCHEOLOGY  ARCTIC & ANTARCTIC

ARMS & ARMOR  ASTRONOMY  AZTEC, INCA & MAYA  BASEBALL  BATTLE  BIBLE LANDS  BIRD

BOAT  BOOK  BUILDING  BUTTERFLY & MOTH  CAR  CASTLE  CAT

CHEMISTRY  COSTUME  COWBOY  CRIME & DETECTION  CRYSTAL & GEM  DANCE  DESERT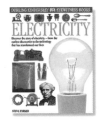

DINOSAUR  DOG  EAGLE & BIRDS OF PREY  EARLY HUMANS  EARTH  ECOLOGY  ELECTRICITY

ELECTRONICS  ELEPHANT  ENERGY  EPIDEMIC  EVEREST  EVOLUTION  EXPLORER

FARM FILM FISH FLAG FLYING MACHINE FORCE & MOTION FOSSIL

FUTURE  GORILLA, MONKEY & APE  HORSE